The Travels
of Marco Polo

Titles in the World History Series

WORLD
HISTORY SERIES ■ ■ ■

The Travels
of Marco Polo

by
Mary Hull

Lucent Books, P.O. Box 289011, San Diego, CA 92198-9011

Library of Congress Cataloging-in-Publication Data

Hull, Mary,
       The Travels of Marco Polo / by Mary Hull.
       p. cm.—(World history series)
       Includes bibliographical references and index.
          ISBN 1-56006-238-X (acid-free)
       1. Polo, Marco, 1254-1323?—Journeys—Juvenile
literature.   2. Voyages and travels—Juvenile literature.
3. Explorers—Italy—Biography—Juvenile literature.
4. China—Description and travel—Juvenile literature.
[1. Polo, Marco, 1254-1323? 2. Explorers. 3. Voyages
and travels.]   I. Title.   II. Series.
       G370.P9H84   1995
915.04'2—dc20   94-2924
                                                                    CIP
                                                                     AC

Copyright 1995 by Lucent Books, Inc., P.O. Box 289011,
San Diego, California, 92198-9011

Printed in the U.S.A.

Contents

Foreword

Each year on the first day of school, nearly every history teacher faces the task of explaining why his or her students should study history. One logical answer to this question is that exploring what happened in our past explains how the things we often take for granted—our customs, ideas, and institutions—came to be. As statesman and historian Winston Churchill put it, "Every nation or group of nations has its own tale to tell. Knowledge of the trials and struggles is necessary to all who would comprehend the problems, perils, challenges, and opportunities which confront us today." Thus, a study of history puts modern ideas and institutions in perspective. For example, though the founders of the United States were talented and creative thinkers, they clearly did not invent the concept of democracy. Instead, they adapted some democratic ideas that had originated in ancient Greece and with which the Romans, the British, and others had experimented. An exploration of these cultures, then, reveals their very real connection to us through institutions that continue to shape our daily lives.

Another reason often given for studying history is the idea that lessons exist in the past from which contemporary societies can benefit and learn. This idea, although controversial, has always been an intriguing one for historians. Those that agree that society can benefit from the past often quote philosopher George Santayana's famous statement, "Those who cannot remember the past are condemned to repeat it." Historians who ascribe to Santayana's philosophy believe that, for example, studying the events that led up to the major world wars or other significant historical events would allow society to chart a different and more favorable course in the future.

Just as difficult as convincing students to realize the importance of studying history is the search for useful and interesting supplementary materials that present historical events in a context that can be easily understood. The volumes in Lucent Books' World History Series attempt to present a broad, balanced, and penetrating view of the march of history. Ancient Egypt's important wars and rulers, for example, are presented against the rich and colorful backdrop of Egyptian religious, social, and cultural developments. The series engages the reader by enhancing historical events with these cultural contexts. For example, in *Ancient Greece*, the text covers the role of women in that society. Slavery is discussed in *The Roman Empire*, as well as how slaves earned their freedom. The numerous and varied aspects of everyday life in these and other societies are explored in each volume of the series. Additionally, the series covers the major political, cultural, and philosophical ideas as the torch of civilization is passed from ancient Mesopotamia and Egypt, through Greece, Rome, Medieval Europe, and other world cultures, to the modern day.

The material in the series is formatted in a thorough, precise, and organized manner. Each volume offers the reader a comprehensive and clearly written overview of an important historical event or period. The topic under discussion is placed in a broad, historical context. For example, *The Italian Renaissance* begins with a discussion of the High Middle Ages and the loss of central control that allowed certain Italian cities to develop artistically. The book ends by looking forward to the Reformation and interpreting the societal changes that grew out of the Renaissance. Thus, students are not only involved in an historical era, but also enveloped by the events leading up to that era and the events following it.

One important and unique feature in the World History Series is the primary and secondary source quotations that richly supplement each volume. These quotes are useful in a number of ways. First, they allow students access to sources they would not normally be exposed to because of the difficulty and obscurity of the original source. The quotations range from interesting anecdotes to far-sighted cultural perspectives and are drawn from historical witnesses both past and present. Second, the quotes demonstrate how and where historians themselves derive their information on the past as they strive to reach a consensus on historical events. Lastly, all of the quotes are footnoted, familiarizing students with the citation process and allowing them to verify quotes and/or look up the original source if the quote piques their interest.

Finally, the books in the World History Series provide a detailed launching point for further research. Each book contains a bibliography specifically geared toward student research. A second, annotated bibliography introduces students to all the sources the author consulted when compiling the book. A chronology of important dates gives students an overview, at a glance, of the topic covered. Where applicable, a glossary of terms is included.

In short, the series is designed not only to acquaint readers with the basics of history, but also to make them aware that their lives are a part of an ongoing human saga. Perhaps they will then come to the same realization as famed historian Arnold Toynbee. In his monumental work, *A Study of History*, he wrote about becoming aware of history flowing through him in a mighty current, and of his own life "welling like a wave in the flow of this vast tide."

Important Dates in the History of the Travels of Marco Polo

1200	1220	1240	1260	1280	1300	1320	1340

1204
Crusaders sack Constantinople, establishing Latin Christian rule.

1206
Genghis Khan is declared supreme monarch of the Mongols.

1215
Mongols defeat Ch'in Empire in northern China and capture Peking.

1245
Pope Innocent IV sends Friar Giovanni di Plano Carpini to convert the Mongols.

1253
William of Rubrick is sent on a mission to the Mongols by Louis IX of France.

1254
Marco Polo is born in Venice, Italy.

1256
Kublai Khan becomes ruler of the Mongol Empire.

1260
Niccolo and Maffeo Polo begin their first trading journey to the East.

1269
Polo brothers return to Venice from the court of Kublai Khan.

1271
Pope Gregory X is elected; Marco accompanies Niccolo and Maffeo as they begin their return journey to the court of Kublai Khan.

1275
Marco, Niccolo, and Maffeo arrive at Shang-tu, the Mongolian summer capital.

1275-1292
Polos are members of the court of Kublai Khan; Marco serves as roving ambassador.

1295
Marco, Niccolo, and Maffeo return to Venice after an absence of twenty-four years.

1298-1299
Marco is captured at the naval battle of Curzola and imprisoned in Genoa; dictates *A Description of the World* to cell mate Rustichello.

1307
Pope Clement V forbids all trading with Muslims; Charles de Valois, brother of Philip IV of France, requests copy of Marco's manuscript.

| 1360 | 1380 | 1400 | 1420 | 1440 | 1460 | 1480 | 1500 |

1324
Marco Polo dies in Venice at age seventy.

1337
France and England begin the Hundred Years' War.

1347-1351
The Black Death kills one-third of Europe's population.

1351
Laurentian Atlas, with Marco's descriptions of Asian geography, is completed.

1356
Turks take Gallipoli; trade routes to East are blocked by Turks.

1368
Chinese recapture China from the Mongols; Ming dynasty begins.

1375
Catalan Atlas, showing Central Asia and China as described by Marco Polo, is completed.

1455
Johannes Gutenberg invents the printing press.

1477
First edition of *A Description of the World* is printed at Nuremberg.

1488
Bartholomeu Diaz sails around the Cape of Good Hope, near the southern tip of Africa.

1492
Christopher Columbus tries to reach Japan but ends up making the European discovery of the New World.

1497
Vasco da Gama sails to India.

Forerunner of an International Age

In 1295, after a twenty-four-year absence from Europe, Marco Polo, his father Niccolo, and his uncle Maffeo had difficulty finding their old home in Venice. The three ragged, tanned, and Tatar-dressed men had been traveling overland and by sea from China for three and a half years. They had finally arrived in their own city, but by now they had nearly forgotten how to speak their native tongue; years of conversing in foreign dialects made it difficult for them to recover their Venetian accents and phrases.

With Niccolo and Maffeo, who were merchants, Marco had set sail from Venice in 1271 for the court of the Mongol emperor Kublai Khan. Their journey took them by sea and overland on the Silk Road and other trade routes established across Central Asia. Marco was only seventeen when he began this long series of adventures with his father and his uncle, and now he was returning to his birthplace as a forty-one-year-old stranger. The men were headed for the home they had left, which they had heard was now occupied by distant members of the Polo family.

When they arrived at the once familiar doorway, the Polos found themselves unable to enter. Relatives turned them away, refusing to believe that they were the long-lost Polos. Marco, Niccolo, and Maffeo

The Polos observed strange new worlds as they traveled through Asia seeking increased trade and commerce.

had been given up for dead decades earlier when news of them had ceased to reach Venice. The Polos had ventured so far east into the Asian continent that they met no other Westerners in their travels.

The three men demanded the chance to prove their identity, but the door was shut in their faces. When Marco, Niccolo, and Maffeo forced their way in, the frightened occupants of the house sent for other family members to help them repel the unwelcome visitors, who might have been intent on robbery. According to legend, the travelers devised a plan that would establish their identity and convince the skeptical family of their sincerity. They invited all their relatives to a banquet honoring their return. When the dinner was over and the food cleared from the table, the Polos left the room and returned in the worn travel outfits they had arrived in. Then taking small knives, they began to rip open the seams and linings of their garments, out of which fell diamonds, rubies, sapphires, emeralds, and a rainbow of other gems. Before leaving the court of Kublai Khan, the men had traded the gold and other bulky possessions they had accumulated for jewels, which were much easier to handle and protect during the long journey home.

Skeptics

This fabulous display of wealth convinced everyone that the three men were really the long-lost Polo merchants. News of their return from the East with so many treasures spread rapidly. But the people of Venice were not able to accept all the Polos had to say about the East, and some of the strange travel tales Marco told made people think he was lying. At that time, Europeans knew very little about the East, and some Eastern practices and customs such as the burning of black stones (coal) for fuel, the use of paper money, and the eating of nuts as large as a man's head

(coconuts) were so foreign to Europeans that they refused to consider the possibility that they might be true.

But Marco felt it was his duty to inform people about what he had seen. On their voyage home he had told his father, "It must be God's pleasure that we return to Venice to tell people of all the things the world contains."[1] In 1298 Marco completed a book called *A Description of the World*, which introduced many foreign cultures and traditions into the libraries and minds of European readers. In an age when Europeans tended to fear foreigners or to regard them with suspicion, Marco's book portrayed people in the East as interested in the West and friendly toward Europe.

A page from Marco Polo's Description of the World, *which was widely read in Europe after its completion in 1298.*

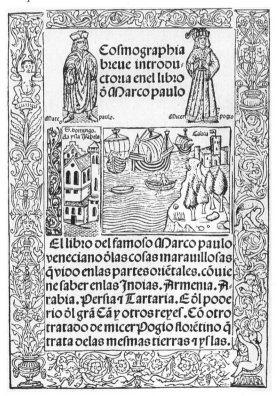

Marco Polo was a forerunner of an international age: He spoke several languages and dialects, interacted with many people of diverse and foreign backgrounds, and kept an open mind toward cultures and religions unlike his own while acting as Europe's unofficial emissary to the East as well as an ambassador of the Mongol Empire. Marco Polo's descriptions of his travels also inspired other explorers and merchants to follow in his footsteps, and it was his geographic knowledge of Asia that provided them with directions.

Since European maps of Asia in Marco Polo's day were based on guesswork or biblical legend, the average European did not have an accurate conception of world geography. Marco's *Description of the World* became an invaluable contribution to the body of European geographic knowledge. The book told of the Pacific Ocean, east of Asia, in addition to the Atlantic, west of Spain and England. In his book Marco also estimated the size of Japan and China and the number of islands in the Pacific Ocean. Two important sets of maps from the fourteenth century reflect the changes Marco Polo's book brought to Western geography: the Laurentian Atlas of 1351 and the Catalan Atlas of 1375. Both of these maps depict Central Asia, China, and Japan as described by Polo, and both are attempts to produce real physical geography, not biblical lore.

Before Marco's book was written, geographers had no idea of the size or extent of the Asian landmass. In fact, it was Marco Polo's estimate of its great size that inspired a later explorer, Christopher

Marco Polo became famous for his travels across the Asian landmass. His discoveries increased geographical knowledge and spurred exploration of distant lands.

Columbus, to believe it possible to reach the East by sailing west. When Christopher Columbus landed in North America in 1492 he had with him letters from Ferdinand and Isabella of Spain addressed to the "Great Khan of Cathay," and on board his ship he carried a heavily annotated copy of Marco's *Description of the World*. Marco Polo's journey and the subsequent publication of his book not only increased Europe's geographic and cultural knowledge of the East, they also stimulated exploration to the West that led to the first European voyages to the New World.

1 A World in Transition

When Marco was born into the Polo family of Venice in 1254, Italy was not yet Italy; it was a collection of city-states, of which Venice, Pisa, and Genoa were the most prominent. Marco's father, Niccolo, and his uncle Maffeo, Venetian merchants specializing in the jewel trade, were also noblemen with seats on the Great Council, the representative assembly of the Venetian republic. Venice, Pisa, and Genoa were rivals in the importation to Europe of such luxury goods as jewels, spices, and cloth, especially silk. Venice was the most powerful of the Italian city-states because of its influence in Constantinople, the city at the gateway to the Black Sea and the Middle East. A thirteenth-century French Crusade, aided by the Venetian naval fleet, had captured Constantinople from the Arabs and sacked the city. When the French installed their emperor at Constantinople, Venice shared in some of the booty and advantage of this maneuver. Venetians were allowed to settle in Constantinople, which gave them an advantage over the Pisans and Genoese when trading with the Middle East, for the Black Sea virtually became, in the words of one

Venice, a powerful Italian city-state. In Marco Polo's day, Venice was a wealthy, beautiful city, bustling with commerce and trade.

A City in Love with Trade

The Venice the Polos left behind in the mid-thirteenth century was at its zenith of power and wealth. The medieval writer Martino Da Canale lived in Venice during the Polos' lifetimes, and he may have known Marco as a young boy. Henry Hart's Marco Polo: Venetian Adventurer *contains Da Canale's descriptions of the wealth of the city of Venice.*

"Venice is today the most beautiful and the pleasantest city in all the world, full of beauty and of all good things. Merchandise flows through this noble city even as the water flows through it and about it and in all places, save in the houses and on the streets, and when the citizens go forth, they can return to their homes either by sea or by the streets. From every place come merchandise and merchants, who buy the merchandise as they will and cause it to be taken to their own countries. Within this city is found food in great abundance, bread and wine, chickens and river fowls, meat, both fresh and salt, the great fish both of the sea and of the rivers, and merchants of every country who sell and buy. You may find in plenty within this beautiful city men of good breeding, old and middle-aged and young, much to be praised for their noble character, and merchants who sell and buy, and money changers and citizens of every craft, and seafaring men of every sort, and vessels to carry [goods] to every port, and galleys to destroy their enemies. Moreover, in this beautiful city are fair ladies and damsels and young maidens in great number, and apparelled [dressed] very richly."

historian, "a Venetian lake."[2] Because an active jewel trade was carried on at Constantinople, Niccolo and Maffeo Polo maintained a home there to use while on trading ventures.

Europe had carried on an active trade with the East since silk was first imported from China to the Roman Empire in 1 B.C. For centuries, European merchants had been trading woolen and linen textiles, glass, precious stones, and fragrant gums for luxury items from India and the Far East: silk, spices, perfume, incense, precious gems, and drugs of all kinds. A tremendous demand existed for these products in Europe, especially among the nobility. But European merchants purchased Eastern wares through Middle Eastern merchants, rather than attempting such a voyage themselves. The overland route to China was populated by various warring peoples, and travel to the Far East was arduous and dangerous. For centuries little formal contact between Europe and the Far East had been attempted.

One of the reasons for this lack of communication was the hostility between Christian Europe and the Muslim, or Is-

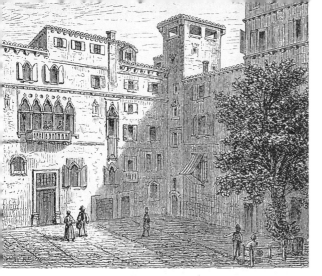

Marco Polo's home in Venice.

ercise its power and control in other parts of the world. Church leaders and many Christian rulers of Europe were especially concerned because the Muslims occupied the Holy Land: the city of Jerusalem and the surrounding Middle Eastern lands where Jesus was born and had lived. Through the influence of the church, the rulers of Europe became involved in the Crusades, armed expeditions aimed at liberating the Holy Land from the Muslims.

lamic, powers in the Middle East. When Marco Polo was a boy in the 1260s, the one power that managed to unite the countries of Europe was the Catholic Church, headed by the pope in Rome. During the Middle Ages, the church had created a body of orthodox doctrines stating its position and its ideas about the world. Anyone who opposed the doctrines of the church was subject to be labeled a heretic and punished, sometimes even tortured or put to death. The church had become a powerful institution, itching to ex-

Rise of a Christian Worldview

The growth of a Christian worldview in the Middle Ages also caused what historian Daniel Boorstin has referred to as "the great interruption of geographic knowledge."[3] The most accurate sources on Eastern geography, the classical works of Herodotus (fifth century B.C.) and Ptolemy (second century A.D.), were discarded and ignored during the Middle Ages because they did not conform to Christian theology, which based geography on bibli-

The papal court is depicted in a thirteenth-century manuscript. When Polo was a boy, the Catholic Church was a powerful institution. Geographical data had to conform to the teachings of the church.

cal legend and prophecies even when the physical reality was different. For example, because the prophet Ezekiel wrote, "Thus saith the Lord God; this is Jerusalem: I have set it in the midst of the nations and countries that are round about her," Christian maps placed Jerusalem at the center of the earth.[4] The maps also included the Garden of Eden and the Tower of Babel. Many historians believe that while the Arabs and the Chinese were developing the art of cartography, or mapmaking, and expanding their geographic knowledge, European progress in this area was impeded by the rigidity of church authorities. As a consequence, European explorers like the Polos did not have a very good idea of what the Far East was like or the best route to use to travel there, nor did they know what to expect once they reached the East. At the time of the Polos, Europe knew little about the Mongol Empire, one of the largest, most highly organized empires in world history. Soon, however, it would become first the Polos' destination, then Marco's base from which to explore the East.

The Mongol Empire

In the mid-thirteenth century, while European kings distanced themselves from the papacy and the church underwent a rapid succession of ineffective leaders (there were five popes during Marco's lifetime), the Mongol Empire was growing. The Mongols had begun their conquest of Asian lands under the leadership of Genghis Khan in 1206, and by 1260 their empire included two-thirds of the Eurasian landmass, extending from the

Genghis Khan organized the nomadic Mongol tribes into a unified fighting force. Under Genghis Khan, the Mongol Empire expanded across Asia until it covered most of the continent.

Arctic to the Himalayan Mountains and including all of China, Mongolia, Afghanistan, Iran, Iraq, and Korea as well as parts of modern Siberia, Russia, Turkey, Syria, Pakistan, India, Vietnam, and Cambodia. The Mongols were fierce warriors, but it was primarily the effective organization of their empire into numerous khanates (kingdoms), ruled by khans (kings) who deferred to the Great Khan, that enabled them to control and maintain their vast network of conquered lands.

Europe was not immune to a Mongol attack. Genghis Khan had been advised that the grazing was better to the west and in 1241, under the direction of his successor, Ogodei Khan, the Mongol army in-

The Army That Astonished Europe

The success of the Mongol army startled all of Europe. Volume II of H.G. Wells's Outline of History *points out that the accomplishments of the Mongol military were not fully understood until the modern era.*

"It is only recently that European history has begun to understand that the successes of the Mongol army, which overran Poland and occupied Hungary in the spring of A.D. 1241, were won by consummate strategy and were not due to a mere overwhelming superiority of numbers. But this fact has not yet become a matter of common knowledge; the vulgar opinion which represents the Tartars as a wild horde carrying all before them solely by their multitude, and galloping through Eastern Europe without a strategic plan, rushing at all obstacles and overcoming them by mere weight, still prevails. . . .

It was wonderful how punctually and effectually the arrangements of the [Mongol] commander were carried out in operations extending from the Lower Vistula to Transylvania. Such a campaign was quite beyond the power of any European army of the time, and it was beyond the vision of any European commander. There was no general in Europe, from Frederick II downward, who was not an amateur in strategy compared to Ogodei. It should also be noticed that the Mongols embarked upon the enterprise with full knowledge of the political situation of Hungary and the condition of Poland—they had taken care to inform themselves by a well-organized system of spies; on the other hand, the Hungarians and Christian powers, like childish barbarians, knew hardly anything about their enemies."

The stone walls of a heavily guarded fortress are no match for the dauntless Mongol army.

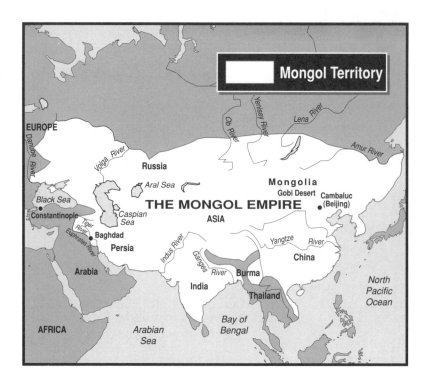

Mongol Territory

EUROPE

Danube River

Volga River

Ob River

Yenisey River

Lena River

Amur River

Russia

Aral Sea

Mongolia

Gobi Desert

Cambaluc
(Beijing)

Black Sea

Constantinople

THE MONGOL EMPIRE

Caspian
Sea

ASIA

Tigris River

Euphrates River

Baghdad

Persia

Indus River

Ganges River

Yangtze River

China

Arabia

Burma

North
Pacific
Ocean

India

Thailand

AFRICA

Arabian
Sea

Bay of
Bengal

(Below) Genghis was succeeded by his son Ogodei (seated on throne). Under Ogodei, the Mongols stormed across Europe, pillaging cities and slaughtering all who crossed their path. (Right) The Mongol Empire at its peak.

vaded eastern Europe. The Russian city of Kiev fell under attack, and according to a Russian account of the event, the Mongols were merciless:

> The inhabitants were, without regard to age or sex, slaughtered with the savage cruelty of the Mongol revenge; some were impaled, some shot at with arrows for sport, others were flayed or had nails or splinters driven under their nails. Priests were roasted alive, and nuns and maidens ravished in the churches before their relatives. No eye remained open to weep for the dead.[5]

The Mongols went on to attack Poland and Hungary, then advanced to the borders of the territories of modern Austria and southern Germany, where they were on the verge of conquering the rest of Europe when suddenly they withdrew to Karakorum, their capital. Trembling Euro-

A City of Fantastic Riches Is Robbed

Constantinople was a city of great, almost indescribable wealth. Rabbi Benjamin of Tudela in Navarre traveled through the city just a few years before it was pillaged by the crusaders and the Latins, and his record of the city can be found in Henry Hart's biography, Venetian Adventurer.

"The circumference of the city of Constantinople is eighteen miles. . . . Great stir and bustle prevail in Constantinople in consequence of the conflux of many merchants, who resort thither, both by land and by sea, from all parts of the world for purposes of trade. . . . At Constantinople is the place of worship called St. Sophia. . . . It contains as many altars as there are days of the year, and possesses innumerable riches. . . . It is ornamented with pillars of gold and silver, and with innumerable lamps of the same precious metals. . . . King Manuel had built a large palace for his residence on the seashore. . . . The pillars and walls are covered with pure gold, and all the wars of the ancients, as well as his own wars, are represented in pictures. The throne in this palace is of gold, and ornamented with precious stones. . . . The tribute [payments from cities under Constantinople's protection], which is brought to Constantinople every year from all parts of Greece, consisting of silks, and purple cloths, and gold, fills many towers. These riches and buildings are equalled nowhere in the world. They say that the tribute of the city alone amounts every day to twenty thousand florins (100,000 gold francs) arising from rents of hostelries and bazaars and from the duties of merchants who arrive by sea and by land. The Greeks . . . are extremely rich, and possess great wealth in gold and precious stones. . . . They dress in garments of silk, ornamented with gold and other valuable materials. . . . The Greeks have soldiers of all nations, whom they call barbarians, for the purpose of carrying on their wars. . . . They have no martial spirit themselves, and, like women, are unfit for warlike purposes."

peans regarded this retreat as a miracle from God. Actually, however, the Mongols had turned around because they had received word of the death of the Great Khan, Ogodei. Everyone wanted to attend the conference at which his successor would be chosen.

As soon as Christendom heard accounts of the Mongol onslaught in Russia and eastern Europe, leaders began planning for a Mongol invasion. In 1245 Pope Innocent IV convened a special council in Lyons, France, to "find a remedy for the Tartars and other spurners of the faith and persecutors of the people of Christ."[6] (Europeans often mistakenly referred to Mongols and other Asian peoples as Tartars instead of Tatars, who are Mongolian people named after the Chinese word "ta-ta," which means nomad. Perhaps because of the Mongols' ferocity, Europeans associated the name "Tatar" with "Tartarus," the Greek word for hell.) Though Pope Innocent's predecessor, Pope Gregory IX, had called for a Crusade against the Mongols, no one had responded to this warning. Now the danger of a Mongol invasion was imminent. The Lyons council begged all Christian people to prepare for a Mongol attack by blocking the roads along Europe's borders with ditches, walls, or buildings.

Muslims in Persia and in the eastern Mediterranean region, whose lives and territory were being destroyed by Mongols, sent envoys to the pope's council at Lyons, urging the leaders of Europe to join them in a fight against the Mongols. But Europe preferred to try to make an alliance with the Mongols against the Muslims. Christian officials refused to help the Muslims, whom they believed to be heretics and therefore the worst of their enemies. Mongols, being merely heathens, were potential converts to Christianity, hence potential allies. The bishop of Winchester suggested that Europe "let dog bite dog."[7] That is, he hoped the Mongols and Muslims would kill each other off, ridding Europe of both problems.

Europe did attempt to convert the Mongols, though. In 1246 Giovanni di Plano Carpini, a Franciscan friar dispatched by Pope Innocent IV, reached the Mongol capital of Karakorum with letters from the pope asking the Mongols to become Christians. The Great Khan of the Mongols at that time was Guyug Khan, a grandson of Genghis Khan, and he made the following response to this Christian overture:

The series of your letters contained advice that we ought to be baptized

---

A Bloodthirsty Army

In Chronica Majora, *quoted by Sir Percy Sykes in* The Quest for Cathay, *the English monk Matthew Paris describes the Mongol onslaught on eastern Europe.*

"In this year [1240] a detestable nation of Satan, to wit the countless army of the Tartars, broke loose from its mountain-environed home, and, piercing the solid rocks of the Caucasus mountains, poured forth like devils. . . . They are thirsting for and drinking blood, tearing and devouring the flesh of dogs and men, dressed in ox-hides, armed with plates of iron, thickset, strong, invincible."

and become Christians; we briefly reply that we do not understand why we ought to do so. . . . You Christians believe that you only are Christians and despise others; but how do you know on whom God may choose to bestow his favor? We adore God, and, in his strength, will overwhelm the whole earth from the East to the West. But if we were not men strengthened by God, what could we do? . . . Whoever recognizes and submits to the Great Khan will be saved, whoever refuses submission will be wiped out.[8]

In 1253 another Franciscan friar, called William of Rubrick, was sent by his king, Louis IX of France, to Karakorum. This attempt to convert the Mongols also failed, making European leaders even more wary of a potential invasion from the East.

Mongols Reopen the Trade Routes

Though the Mongols terrified Europe with the possibility of an invasion, Europe did benefit from the strength of the Mongol Empire. The Mongols conquered the Muslims and plundered their capital city of Baghdad in 1258, much to the joy of Christendom. In addition, because the Mongols controlled the Middle East and Asia, they reopened trade routes that had long been considered unsafe for European travelers. These trade routes, known as the Silk Road, consisted of a network of caravan tracks, roads, and mountain passes crossing the Eurasian landmass. Niccolo and Maffeo Polo were among the first merchants to take advantage of this relatively stable period.

Venetian merchants had long traded in Constantinople, Turkey, and ports along the Black Sea, but the opening up of the Silk Road routes under the power of the Mongols provided an attractive new opportunity for commerce. So in 1260, when Marco was six, his father and his uncle set out to trade in these newly accessible lands. By traveling off the main trade routes and away from major centers of commerce, they hoped to make a better profit, for they had heard that there was good money to be made by trading furs, hides, salt, pitch, wood, and slaves among the nomads to the north of the Black Sea. They also hoped to establish contacts in Eastern, or Levantine, lands [so called after the French verb "lever," meaning "to rise," in reference to the observation that the sun rises in the east]. Such luxury goods as spices, jewels, incense, and fine cloth could be acquired by trading in the East and sold for a profit in Venice.

The Polo merchants were shrewd businessmen and they ventured farther east than any Venetians before them, but they were not the first Europeans to meet Mongols on Mongol territory. The Franciscan missionary sent by Pope Innocent IV in 1245 had made Europe's first formal contact with the Mongol Empire. Even so, the West's understanding of Eastern lands remained very limited. Niccolo and Maffeo Polo set out on a journey that lasted nine years and took them to foreign and unexpected places. They could not have imagined that their journey would make it possible for Niccolo's young son Marco to one day return with them to China and write *A Description of the World*, which would tell Europe so much about the people, customs, folklore, and geography of Central and Eastern Asia.

2 The First Journey of the Polos

In 1260 Constantinople was an unstable city. Riots frequently broke out in the streets, political upheaval seemed imminent, and the Polo brothers decided to leave. They liquidated their merchandise and invested all the profits in jewels, which were easy to transport and could be traded along the way. From Constantinople they sailed across the Black Sea to the port city of Soldaia on the northern coast, where they had another home. Soon the situation in Constantinople grew so precarious that it was dangerous to try to return to Venice, for bandits and pirates were taking advantage of the disorganized political scene, and neither the sea nor the land near Constantinople nor any cities in the Latin (Western) empire were safe for a Venetian merchant to travel.

Unable to return home and not wanting to be robbed or sacrificed in the course of an insurrection, the Polos decided to travel off the main routes of commerce into the region north of the Black Sea. They had heard of Venetian traders who made a good profit in southern Russia by trading furs, hides, salt, pitch, wood, and slaves to the nomadic Mongolian

Constantinople and its surrounding lands provided no safe havens for Venetian merchants. To avoid the insurrections, bandits, and pirates in the area, the Polos traveled off the main routes and headed for Russia.

The Polo brothers bid farewell to Constantinople.

tribes. The Black Sea coast was one of the most prosperous areas for the slave trade during the Polos' time, when people from Russia, Hungary, the Caucasus, and other regions captured by the Mongols often were taken captive and sold. Slaves were in demand in Europe to take the place of paid servants, and in Egypt male slaves were sought for the Egyptian army. Female slaves were also purchased for harems in the Middle East and as concubines for European men.

In exchange for their trade, the Polos hoped to bring home cereals, grains, hides, and furs to stock their emporium at Soldaia. They had also heard that the Mongolian khans were anxious to pur-

chase jewels. So the Polos took the jewels they had bought in Constantinople, along with other items for barter with the northern tribes, and prepared to travel far from the centers of commercial activity. They packed their wares onto a caravan, purchased transport horses, and started overland into Russia toward the court of the nearest khan. It is unknown whether the Polos brought servants with them from Soldaia or whether they acquired them along the way, as slaves were everywhere available for trade, but they were accompanied by slaves for much of their journey.

The Russian land occupied by the Mongols was known as the territory of the Golden Horde, a vast, treeless region bordered by the Ural Mountains. The ruler of this land was Barka Khan, one of the grandsons of Genghis. Here the Polos camped with bands of Mongols who wandered the plains in search of grass and water for their horses. It was said of these people that their "fatherland is their tent and the back of their horses."[9] The Mongols lived in round or six-sided tents called yurts—permanent homes, which could be as large as twenty feet in diameter. The yurts were collapsible, however, and could be folded up and easily transported in carts. They were made from skins or felt coated with tallow and cow's milk to keep the rain from soaking through. This covering was tied to a lightweight wooden frame by leather thongs or horsehair cord. The Polos grew accustomed to sleeping in the yurts, around the fire of dried horse dung that was prepared in the center so the smoke could rise through a hole in the roof. As they traveled among the horde, the Polos also became familiar with the staples of the Mongol diet—dried salted meat and koumiss, an alcoholic drink made from fermented mare's milk.

Though the Polos at first spoke no Mongol, they managed to find food and shelter and to travel successfully among the people they encountered. Trade is a universal language, and the Polos were able to barter wherever they went, trading skins and salt or furs for food. They began to pick up key Mongol words and phrases, and to learn how the Mongols lived and worked. The Polos soon discovered it was a religious custom among the Mongols not to bathe or to wash their clothes. "They never wash their clothes, since they say God would punish them for polluting the water; nor do they hang them up to dry in order not to pollute the air, and they believe it would thunder if they did

As the Polos traveled through Mongol territory, they became accustomed to life in a Mongol camp. The Mongols lived in felt tents called yurts.

Henry Hart's biography Marco Polo: Venetian Adventurer *contains Spanish writer Pero Tafur's description of a slave market in the city of Kaffa, the center of the slave trade when Maffeo and Niccolo Polo were merchants.*

"In this city [Kaffa] they sell more slaves both male and female, than anywhere else in the world. . . . I bought there two female slaves and a male, whom I still have in Cordova with their children. The selling takes place as follows. The sellers make the slaves strip to the skin, males as well as females, and they put on them a cloak of felt, and the price is named. Afterward they throw off their coverings, and make them walk up and down to show whether they have any bodily defect. If there is a Tartar man or woman among them, the price is a third more, since it may be taken as a certainty that no Tartar ever betrayed a master."

so, to show God's displeasure."[10] Only newborn babies were given baths.

Seven days after the child's birth, the family teapot was rinsed, the water used for this purpose was salted, and the baby washed with it. Seven days later he received a bath of salt water. At the end of the third seven days he was washed in diluted milk. Finally, twenty-eight days after birth, he was bathed in his mother's milk to prevent skin trouble. And with these quadruple washings the Mongol is contented for the rest of his life.[11]

As the Polos traveled among the Golden Horde, they passed men making wooden frameworks for their yurts, stitching leather for bridles and saddles, or making arrows. The women tanned skins with ashes and salt, or made felt by beating wet sheep's wool until it clung together and then tying the pressed strips behind graz-ing ponies to be dragged over the grass, to tangle the fibers and strengthen the felt. When they camped at night, the Polos listened to the Mongols' legends, their stories about horses, and their tales of military conquest.

A Warm Reception

When Niccolo and Maffeo reached the town of Sarai, near the junction of the Kama and Volga rivers, they were received by Barka Khan. The Polos presented the ruler of the Golden Horde with jewels they had bought in Constantinople, for they understood that to be accepted and aided, it was essential to present gifts to important people. Barka Khan was extremely pleased with the precious stones. In exchange for this great show of respect, the Polos were received warmly and given back twice the value of their jewels in goods, which they were able to sell at a profit in the neighboring region.

The khan had palaces at both Sarai and Bulgar, and he alternated between them depending on the season, as was the Mongol custom. Sarai and Bulgar also had markets and temples to various religions, especially Islam (Barka Khan was a convert to Islam). The Polos stayed a year trading in both cities, after which they began preparations for the return trip. It was now the spring of 1262, and the brothers planned to return to Constantinople with merchandise for their store, so they bought some arabas—wagons with two large wheels, capable of fording streams and negotiating deep ruts. The wagons also had roofs made of mats that protected the passengers from the sun and rain.

The Polos were just about to depart when war broke out between Barka Khan and his cousin, Hulagu Khan, from the Persian khanate. Barka and Hulagu had

The Perils of Sea Travel

Legends about sea creatures and their origins abounded among sailors in the Polos' time. In Marco Polo: Venetian Adventurer, *Henry Hart quotes Ludolph Von Suchem's "Description of the Holy Land," written in 1350, which tells of a fish, probably a shark, known to sailors as the "sea-swine."*

"[The sea-swine] is greatly to be feared by small ships, for this same fish seldom or never does any mischief to large ships unless pressed by hunger. Indeed, if the sailors give it bread, it departs, and is satisfied; but if it will not depart, then it may be terrified and put to flight by the sight of a man's angry and terrible face. . . . Howbeit, the man must be exceedingly careful when he is looking at the fish not to be afraid of it, but to stare at it with a bold and terrible countenance, for if the fish sees that the man is afraid it will not depart, but bites and tears the ship as much as it can. . . .

I have diligently inquired of knowing seamen whence these fish come, and they have answered me that in England and Ireland there grow on the seashore exceedingly beauteous trees, which bear fruit like apples. In these apples there is bred a worm, and when the apples are ripe they fall to the ground, are broken in the fall, and the worms fly out, having wings like bees. Those of them who first touch the land become creatures of the air, and fly about with the other fowls of the heavens; but such worms as first touch the water become creatures of the water, and swim like fish."

Hulagu Khan pursues Barka Khan after war broke out between the two feuding leaders. During this bloody conflict, travel routes were unsafe. The Polo brothers changed course, heading east on roundabout routes.

been arguing for some time over who would rule the Levantine Tatars, and now they were engaged in a bloody conflict that brought heavy losses to both sides. The Polos could not return home the way they had come because the Volga River was impassable beyond the city of Ukek, and the caravan routes to the southwest were unsafe to travel in wartime, especially with so much merchandise. Not only did they chance becoming prisoners of war if they tried to return to Soldaia, but they also risked losing their cargo to the armies of bandits who took advantage of the lax protection of the caravan routes during wartime. These outlaw groups, who combed the highways looking for loot, were primarily bands of Hungarians, Rus-

sians, and Turks. They hid during the day and attacked caravan camps at night, stealing goods and killing travelers.

Unable to return home, and believing that the war between the khans would last a long time, Niccolo and Maffeo Polo decided to take a roundabout route to the East, eventually reaching Venice by way of this detour. The Polos had learned some Mongol and a Turkish dialect that was spoken virtually everywhere they had traveled, so they felt comfortable continuing through the empire.

After passing through Ukek, the Polos headed southeast through the land corridor between the Aral and Caspian seas. When they reached the desert, they traded their pack horses for camels, which could handle the arid crossing. The Polo caravan crept over the desert for weeks, passing nothing but Tatar nomads who camped off the desert road with their cattle. Finally they reached the trade center of Bukhara, Persia, which rose from the sands by the banks of the Zaravshah River, a city surrounded by ramparts behind which stood mosques with tiled walls and blue domes. In the center of the city atop a hill stood a castle, from which one could see off into the desert.

An Asian Trading Center in the Thirteenth Century

Bukhara was one of the most spectacular trading centers the world had ever known, and people from every country in Asia traveled there to do business. The shops and bazaars of Bukhara overflowed with Eastern wares, such as silks, porcelain, ivory, spices, and finely wrought metalwork. The region around the city was known as a center of higher learning and was rich in schools, towns, and commerce. Bukhara had been savagely destroyed by Genghis Khan's army in 1220 when the city refused to surrender to the Mongol invaders, but it was later restored under the direction of Organa, widow of Genghis's son Chagatai, who had been the first khan of Central Asia. Though Bukhara's population was decimated during Genghis Khan's raid, it was replenished by an influx of Persians, Afghans, Mongols, Chinese, and Kirghiz following the restoration. Consequently, Bukhara became one of the most culturally diverse cities in Asia, and the Polos could not

People from all over Asia brought their goods to Bukhara, the most important trade center in Asia.

The Polo brothers arrive at Bukhara. Because of conflict in Asia at the time, Bukhara became isolated from mercantile traffic. As merchants, the Polos had little reason to remain in Bukhara, yet they could not safely leave the area.

have come to a better place to be exposed to many different elements of Central and East Asian culture.

The Polo brothers themselves attracted quite a bit of attention in the city, as they were the only Westerners living there. In fact, most of the local people had never seen Europeans before, so the Polos became the objects of much curiosity. During their three-year stay at Bukhara, the Polos learned the customs of Asian commerce, as well as the languages and dialects of the region. The trading language of Bukhara was Persian, and though professional translators were available all over the city, the Polo brothers learned to speak Persian and some Arabic.

During the Polos' stay, however, the city's trade ceased to be transcontinental and became more local, for Bukhara was gradually being sealed off from Asia's trade routes. Bukhara and the surrounding regions were experiencing the effects of all the fighting that had developed after Kublai Khan declared himself emperor in 1256, and the next year moved the Mongol capital to Peking, China. All of Asia had undergone civil and dynastic wars as a result of this shift in power, and the wars had detrimental effects on trade. While the Polos were at Bukhara, Kublai Khan's brother and rival, Aric Buga, invaded the region around the city, interrupting the inward flow of goods from the east. At the same time, Hulagu Khan threatened Bukhara by camping his armies to the northwest of the city, sealing off the trade routes in that direction. In this way Bukhara, once the most important trade center in Asia, became isolated from mercantile traffic. Thus the Polos were stuck in Bukhara. Since they could not travel safely in the war zones, they were forced to wait for the wars between the khans to end.

Escape from Bukhara

While the Polos were biding their time, an imperial messenger from Kublai Khan arrived in Bukhara. The Mongol ruler had heard about the two curious Latin men and wanted to see them for himself. "The Great Khan," the messenger informed the Polos, "has never seen any Latin and is exceedingly desirous to meet one. If you will accompany me to him, I assure you that he will be very glad to see you and will treat you with great honor and great bounty."[12]

The Polos had nothing to lose by accepting this offer, although it meant traveling even farther from home. From a merchant's perspective, since Bukhara had ceased to be a center of much trade, it no longer made sense to remain there. Besides, the situation around Bukhara had grown more dangerous, and the Polos might have to stay there indefinitely if they did not take this opportunity to leave. Moreover, imperial messengers enjoyed special privileges when traveling around the empire. Their golden passports from the Great Khan entitled them to protection no matter where they were, and those who dared harm them were subject to death. Accepting the messenger's offer thus would ensure safe passage from Bukhara. The Polos decided to join the khan's messenger and his party on their return trip to China.

Kublai Khan, a grandson of Genghis Khan. Kublai Khan invited the Polos to travel to his court with imperial messengers who enjoyed special travel privileges. The Polos eagerly accepted this opportunity to leave Bukhara.

The group journeyed overland in horse- and ox-drawn carts without harm or hindrance from any of the warring factions. They traveled on roads maintained by the Mongol Empire, some of which were even paved with bricks. Along certain roads stood post stations paced a day's traveling distance apart, at which the party could exchange horses and stay overnight. The post stations were for the official use of employees of the Great Khan.

The party passed through the trading city of Samarkand, a Persian city of domed and tiled Islamic architecture similar to

The Summer Capital at Shang-tu

Kublai Khan's summer palace included an elaborate park whose interior reflected the khan's interests in hunting, botany, and beautiful surroundings. When Maffeo and Niccolo Polo arrived at Shang-tu in the summer of 1265 it probably looked just as their younger relative described it years later, as quoted here from The Travels, *translated and edited by Ronald Latham.*

"Between the inner and outer walls [of the palace] are stretches of park-land with stately trees. The grass grows up here in abundance, because all the paths are paved and built up fully two cubits above the level of the ground, so that no mud forms on them and no rain-water collects in puddles, but the moisture trickles over the lawns, enriching the soil and promoting a lush growth of herbage. In these parks there is a great variety of game, such as white harts, musk-deer, roebuck, stags, squirrels, and many other beautiful animals. All the area within the walls is full of these graceful creatures, except the paths that people walk on.

On the northern side of the palace, at the distance of a bow-shot but still within the walls, the Great Khan had had made an earthwork, that is to say a mound fully 100 paces in height and over a mile in circumference. This mound is covered with a dense growth of trees, all evergreens that never shed their leaves. And I assure you that whenever the Great Khan hears tell of a particularly fine tree he has it pulled up, roots and all and with a quantity of earth, and transported to this mound by elephants. No matter how big the tree may be, he is not deterred from transplanting it. In this way he had assembled here the finest trees in the world. In addition, he has had the mound covered with lapis lazuli, which is intensely green, so that trees and rock alike are as green as green can be and there is no other color to be seen. . . . On top of this mound, in the middle of the summit, he has a large and handsome palace, and this too is entirely green. And I give you my word that mound and trees and palace form a vision of such beauty that it gladdens the hearts of all beholders. It was for the sake of this entrancing view that the Great Khan had them constructed, as well as for the refreshment and recreation they might afford him."

After a year of travel, the Polo brothers arrive at the court of Kublai Khan. The khan questioned the Polos extensively about life in the Western world.

Bukhara. Next they reached the city of Kashgar, just north of the Himalaya Mountains, and from there the party entered the Gobi desert of China. On the other side of the Gobi, the group traveled to the westernmost reach of the Great Wall of China, which they followed east toward the Mongol summer capital at Shang-tu. All across China the Polos' caravan passed groups of Mongol soldiers with their bows and arrows, spears, shields, and helmets. Some soldiers were in charge of patrolling the imperial roads and clearing out the bandits and robbers who preyed on caravans. The Polos traveled with their imperial escort for a year before finally arriving at the court of the Great Khan.

Kublai Khan was eager to meet the two foreigners; he seemed to be delighted by the Polos' presence in his empire. Moreover the Christian emissaries Giovanni di Plano Carpini and William of Rubrick, who had visited when the Mongol capital was at Karakorum, never traveled inland across China and to the Chinese coast. Thus when the Polos first arrived at the court of Kublai Khan in the 1260s, they were most likely the first Europeans ever seen by people living in that area.

At the Court of Kublai Khan

Kublai Khan took advantage of the Polos' presence and was most anxious to ask them questions about their native country. After providing luxurious accommodations for the Polos and holding a feast in their honor, the Great Khan began to question his guests about Western government, the European kings, and the papacy. Kublai Khan was very curious about the West, and he wanted to know about his political counterparts. By this time, the Polos had learned to speak Mongol so well that they were able to understand and answer the ruler's questions. After the Polos had given the Great Khan an accurate political description of Europe, the various kings, their administrations, and their relations with one another, the Mongol ruler desired to know more about European military prowess, manners, and customs. Next he wanted to know about the pope, and the ideas and practices of the Catholic Church. He was interested in Christianity, and all the other great religions of the world. In fact, Kublai welcomed people of all faiths to his court so that they might try to demonstrate the superiority of their respective religions and persuade the Great Khan to become a convert. Kublai Khan was very curious about Christianity and its power. He asked the Polo brothers if they would act as messengers and assist him in corresponding with the pope.

The Polos quickly realized that there could be no safer way to return to their homeland than as imperial messengers of the Great Khan, for they had already seen the privileges accorded to those who carried the golden seal. They also realized that this favor to Kublai Khan could benefit them by helping them to establish steady trade with the Far East. Thus, the Polos accepted the Great Khan's offer to act as his messengers to the pope, and arrangements were made for their return to the West.

A Religious Overture

Kublai Khan prepared a letter to the pope, which declared his interest in Christianity, and asked the pontiff to send him one hundred educated Christian men who were well-versed in Christian philosophy and in the seven disciplines the Polos had told him represented a medieval education: rhetoric, logic, grammar, arithmetic, astronomy, music, and geometry. Kublai Khan wanted access to that information; if it could be taught to his people, they would know all that Europeans knew. He also told the pope he wanted men who excelled at debate and would be able to prove to his people the superiority of Christianity over all other religions. If they could do this to his satisfaction, the khan wrote, he and all his people would become Christians.

Historians doubt the sincerity of Kublai Khan's stated intention of Christianizing his people; many think that Kublai wanted learned Christian men to help him run his government, not to act as spiritual advisers. The Mongol Empire lacked capable civil servants, since few Mongols were educated. The khan did not trust the Muslims, and the Chinese, who desired to overthrow their Mongol conquerors, were not good candidates for the civil service. Thus the message to the pope was a deliberate attempt to secure Kublai's empire politically, couched as an appeasing religious overture.[13]

The khan entrusted this letter to the Polos and asked them to bring him some of the oil from the Lamp of the Holy Sepulchre, which hung above the cave tomb in Jerusalem where Jesus was believed to have been buried. The lamp, which was kept constantly lit by monks, was believed to be magical. According to legend, it would go out by itself each year on Good Friday, then relight itself on Easter Sunday at the hour of the resurrection. Oil taken from the lamp was supposed to have remarkable curative powers and was one of the most prized items of Middle Eastern trade. Apparently Kublai Khan had heard of the power associated with the lamp.

The Polos were outfitted for their journey and given an imperial escort named Cogotal, who was one of the khan's barons. All three men received golden tablets one foot long and three inches across, inscribed with the khan's order that they be provided with safe travel throughout the empire, as well as all the horses, escorts, provisions, and lodging they required. Violation of this order was punishable by death.

The Polos Return to Europe

In the spring of 1266 the Polos and their caravan began traveling toward the West—and home. Only a few weeks into their journey from the khan's court, however, their escort Cogotal became ill (or pretended to be ill), and the Polos were forced to leave him behind and travel on alone, with only their golden tablets as evidence of their imperial mission. Most likely, the Polos returned to Bukhara via the same roads they had used to arrive at Shang-tu, then headed west toward the Mediterranean Sea, passing by the south-ern tip of the Caspian Sea, and on through Baghdad. The return voyage took three years, for snow, flooding, and muddy conditions caused numerous delays.

In April 1269 the Polos arrived at the city of Acre, on the eastern end of the Mediterranean, just north of Jerusalem. Acre was the last commercial port on the coast of Syria under the control of the crusaders, hence it was occupied by Latins. The Polos immediately visited the Venetian district of the city and caught up on all the news they had missed while abroad. They discovered that Pope Clement IV had died while they were away, and a successor had not yet been elected. They would not be able to complete their mission for the khan until a new pope had been chosen.

Niccolo and Maffeo Polo then set sail for Venice. When they arrived at their old home, they discovered that during their nine-year absence Niccolo's wife had died. Marco Polo, now fifteen, was living with relatives in Venice. He was amazed by the tales told by his father and his uncle, and he pleaded to go with them when they returned to the court of the Great Khan. If it had not been for the initial voyage of Niccolo and Maffeo, Marco would never have had an opportunity to travel so far into Asia and to publish a book about his travels. Indeed, no other member of his generation in Europe had such a chance. Fortunately for the Western world, which would later view the East solely through Marco's eyes, Marco Polo was about to join his kinsmen on their return to China.

3 The Second Journey of the Polos

Maffeo and Niccolo remained in Venice for two years, waiting for the election of a new pope, to appoint the hundred Christian scholars requested by Kublai Khan. Eventually, however, Niccolo and Maffeo, fearing that the khan might think they had abandoned his mission, decided to return to China empty-handed. So in 1271, when Marco was seventeen years old, Niccolo and Maffeo left Venice to honor their mission to the khan, and they took Marco with them.

Sailing out of Venice and into the Adriatic Sea, the Polos followed the common Venetian trade route, passing many Venetian ships on their way. They continued around the tip of Greece and across the Mediterranean Sea to Acre, where they needed to consult with the papal legate, Teobaldo of Piacenza. The papal legate was

In the spring of 1266, the Polos headed west. Three years later, they arrived in Venice, their old home.

The Old Man of the Mountain

Marco Polo heard the story of the murderous sect of the sheikh known as the Old Man of the Mountain from the Persian people, and he included it in his own book. This quote is from a modern translation of The Travels *by Ronald Latham.*

"The Old Man of the Mountain has made in a valley between two mountains the biggest and most beautiful garden that was ever seen, planted with all the finest fruits in the world and containing the most splendid mansions and palaces that were ever seen, ornamented with gold and with likenesses of all that is beautiful on earth, and also four conduits, one flowing with wine, one with milk, one with honey, and one with water. . . . And he gave his men to understand that this garden was Paradise. . . .

The Sheikh kept with him at his court all the youths of the country from twelve years old to twenty, all, that is, who shaped well as men at arms. And this is how he did it. He would give them draughts that sent them to sleep on the spot. Then he had them taken and put in the garden. . . . When they awoke and found themselves in there and saw all the things I have told you of, they believed they were really in Paradise. . . .

And when the Sheikh wanted emissaries to send on some mission of murder, he would administer the drug to as many as he pleased; and while they slept he had them carried into his palace. When these youths awoke and found themselves in the castle within the palace, they were amazed and by no means glad, for the Paradise from which they had come was not a place that they would ever willingly have left. They went forthwith to the Sheikh and humbled themselves before him, as men who believed that he was a great prophet. When he asked them whence they came, they would answer that they came from Paradise, and that was in truth the Paradise of which Muhammed [the prophet of Islam] had told their ancestors; and they would tell their listeners all that they had found there. And the others who heard this and had not been there were filled with a great longing to go to this Paradise; they longed for death so that they might go there."

the pope's representative, and the Polos would have to have his permission to take some oil from the Lamp of the Holy Sepulchre in Jerusalem. Since the Polos had been unable to deliver Kublai Khan's letter to a pope, they were especially anxious to comply with the request for holy oil.

When the Polos arrived at Acre they took lodgings in the Venetian district of the city, which was a bustling area. In 1350 a German named Ludolph Von Suchem visited this city while on a pilgrimage to the Holy Land, and his description of the foreign merchants' quarter of Acre mirrored the place the Polos had been just eighty years earlier:

> There dwelt in Acre the richest merchants under heaven, who were gathered together therein out of all nations; there were Pisans, Genoese, and Lombards. . . . There dwelt therein also exceedingly rich merchants of other nations, for from sunrise to sunset all parts of the world brought merchandise thither, and everything that can be found in the world that is wondrous or strange used to be brought thither because of the nobles and princes who dwelt there. . . . [These princes, kings, and nobility of the crusaders' Latin empire] walked about the streets in royal state, with golden coronets on their heads, each of them like a king, with his knights, his followers, his mercenaries and his retainers, his clothing and his warhorse wondrously bedecked with gold and silver, all vying one with another in beauty and novelty of device, and each man apparelling himself with the utmost care.[14]

The Polos met with the papal legate Teobaldo, who gave them permission to take some holy oil. But after retrieving the oil from the Holy Sepulchre in Jerusalem, the Polos returned to Acre and expressed their misgivings to Teobaldo: "We can see that the election of a new Pope is continually being delayed, and we would like to return to the Great Khan, for we are beginning to feel that we have waited too long."[15] Teobaldo sympathized with them and prepared some letters for Kublai, stating that under the circumstances the Polos had done all they could do to complete their mission. He explained how the College of Cardinals had failed to elect a new pope, adding that when the next pontiff had been chosen, Kublai would be notified and his request could be presented to the new church leader.

A New Pope

When the Polos set out on the first overland part of their journey back to China, they were delayed by roadblocks that had been set up by warring factions in the region. While they waited for the roads to reopen, a messenger arrived to announce that the cardinals had chosen Teobaldo himself as the new pope. The messenger said that if the Polos would not mind turning back, Teobaldo (who was now called Pope Gregory X) wished to supply them with missionaries for the khan. The Polos had no trouble returning to Acre, since they were now papal ambassadors. Indeed, the king of Armenia arranged for the Polos to return to Acre on one of his armed galleons.

At Acre the Polos prostrated themselves before Gregory and congratulated him on his accession to the highest office in Christendom. Gregory picked two Dominican, preaching friars, to accompany the Polos on their journey and to teach the Mongols the ways of Christianity. The friars were authorized by Gregory to act as his representatives, and he gave them the power to ordain priests and bishops, and to give or withhold forgiveness of sins. These two men were hardly the "one hundred learned men" requested by Kublai Khan, but the new pope seems to have had difficulty finding qualified men who were willing to travel to the Mongol Empire.

Gregory gave the Polos a personal message for the khan, and he prepared many costly gifts for the emperor, including jewels and crystal vases. Gregory was interested in improving diplomatic relations between the Christian West and the Mongol Empire, so he also wrote a letter to the khan of the Levantine Tatars, asking safe passage for Christian travelers in Middle Eastern territory. Finally, Gregory entrusted the Polos with finding out all they could about the Christian sects that were rumored to exist in Asia.

Journey Back to China

With these gifts and letters, the Polos and the friars embarked on their mission. They sailed back to the coastal city of Ayas, in Armenia, and resumed their overland trek, but soon they encountered another obstacle. The sultan of Egypt, a Mamluk named Bundukari, had invaded Armenia with a large army, creating chaos in the region and making travel conditions entirely unpredictable.

The Mamluks were members of a politically powerful Egyptian military class, and long-range raiding was their specialty. Since the elder Polos were accustomed to finding their way blocked and had experience in making detours to avoid war zones, the conditions created by the Mamluk invasion did not deter them. But the friars, who may not have been enthusiastic about the mission to the Mongols anyway, used the uncertain situation as an excuse for deserting the enterprise. Claiming that they were too afraid for their own safety to

The Polos kneel before Teobaldo after he is named pope. The Polos had promised the khan that they would assist him in corresponding with the pope.

Pope Gregory X outfitted the Polos with supplies and gifts for their long, arduous journey to the Mongol Empire.

the actual journey, it was the notes Marco took that had such a tremendous impact on history. Because Marco decided it would be fun to keep records, and because he later had the opportunity to transcribe these notes into a travel book, medieval Europe learned something of Asia and became intent on exploring that portion of the world. Marco's descriptions were detailed and provided much information about Asia under Mongol rule. As Marco traveled through Central Asia, he described the Armenians, Turks, and Tatars, mentioning in particular that people lived together under the yoke of the Mongol Empire but were free to practice many different religions.

Religious Tolerance in the Mongol Empire

"These [Mongols] do not care what God is worshipped in their territories," Marco wrote later in *Description of the World*.

> So long as all their subjects are loyal and obedient to the Khan and accordingly pay the tribute imposed on them and justice is well observed, you may do as you please about your soul. They object to your speaking ill of their souls or intermeddling with their practices. But concerning God and your own soul do what you will, whether you be Jew or pagan, Saracen or Christian, who live among the Mongols.[16]

The religious tolerance of the Mongols may have been a policy necessary for political survival; considering how many different cultures and regions were encompassed under the Mongol Empire, an attempt to impose a single religion might

continue the journey, the Dominicans handed over the papal letters to the Polos and went back to Acre at the first opportunity. The Polos were powerless to stop them. The desertion of the friars meant that the Polos would have little to show for their journey, but Niccolo and Maffeo wanted to honor their mission to the khan, and they decided to continue.

From Armenia the Polos took a wide detour to the Caucasus Mountains in the north to avoid the Mamluk war zone, then turned south again to western Persia. Marco had brought notebooks with him, and as they traveled through different regions he took notes describing what he saw and recording the stories he heard. More than

The Caliph and His Treasure

When Hulagu Khan captured Baghdad from the Muslims in 1258, the caliph (ruler) of Baghdad was one of the richest men in the world. Marco Polo tells the legend of what happened to the caliph and his treasure in his book, A Description of the World, *also known as* The Travels of Marco Polo. *It is excerpted here from Ronald Latham's translation.*

"The Caliph was captured together with the city [of Baghdad]. After his capture a tower was discovered, filled with gold. When Hulagu saw this he was amazed and ordered the Caliph to be brought before him. 'Caliph,' said he, 'why have you heaped up all this treasure? What did you mean to do with it? Did you not know that I was your enemy and was coming against you with all this host to despoil you? Knowing this, why did you not take your treasure and give it to knights and hired soldiers to defend you and your city?'

The Caliph made no answer because he did not know what to say. Then Hulagu said: 'Caliph, since I see that you love treasure so dearly, I will give you your own to eat.' Next he ordered that the Caliph should be taken and put in the treasure tower and that nothing should be given him to eat or drink. 'Now Caliph,' he said, 'eat your fill of treasure, since you are so fond of it; for you will get nothing else.' After that he left him in the tower, where at the end of four days he died.

So it would have been better indeed for the Caliph if he had given away his treasure to defend his land and his people rather than die bereft of everything. And since then there has been no other Caliph."

The caliph is locked up in his treasure tower, where at the end of four days he died.

have provoked great resistance and even rebellion. The religious tolerance of the Mongols may also have been the result of an enlightened belief that there were many ways to worship God. Kublai Khan's brother, Mangu Khan, said to a Christian missionary in 1254:

> As God hath given the hand many fingers, so hath he given many ways to men. God hath given the Scriptures to you Christians. . . . To us he has given soothsayers, and we do that which they bid us, and we live in peace.[17]

Traditional Mongol religion involved the worship of a sky-spirit and other spirits, as well as ritual fortune-telling. Whatever its rationale, the religious tolerance of the Mongols differed dramatically from the ideas of thirteenth-century European rulers. The Polos observed many different religious sects in the Mongol Empire, including Buddhists, Muslims, Taoists, and Nestorian Christians. Nestorian Christianity was not the same as the Roman Christianity the Polos knew; Nestorians entertained both Asian and Christian beliefs in a mixture that was considered heathen by the Western church. Nevertheless, the Western church was interested in learning more about Asian Christianity, as evidenced when Gregory X asked the Polos to report to him about the Nestorian sect. The Polos appear to have taken this assignment seriously, for the book Marco published years later contained numerous references to Christian sects and to tales of Christian miracles and triumphs over the Muslims in the Middle East.

The Polos Cross Asia to the Persian Gulf

While in Greater Armenia, Marco Polo described Mount Ararat, atop which he claimed could be seen the remains of Noah's Ark, although he added that it was impossible to climb Ararat because of the

Marco was a keen observer of the world around him. Besides leaving vivid descriptions about the peoples and cultures he encountered, Marco left detailed notes about geographical sites, such as Mount Ararat.

snow that covered it winter and summer. Marco also observed, in Russia, the harvesting and use of petroleum—which was not common in Europe at the time but would later become an integral part of the industrialization of society. He wrote that in the Caucasus Mountains of Georgia,

> there is a spring from which gushes a stream of oil, in such abundance that a hundred camels may load there at once. This oil is not good to eat; but it is good for burning and as a salve for men and camels affected with itch or scab. Men come from a long distance to fetch this oil, and in all the neighborhood no other oil is burnt but this.[18]

As the Polos turned southeast toward Persia they entered the province of Mosul (now Iraq). Arabs and Nestorian Christians lived in this region, which was known for its export of the sheer cloth called muslin. From Baghdad, the Polos traveled by horseback and in carts to the trade center of Tabriz, which Marco noted as a city offering good profits to traveling merchants. Though Niccolo and Maffeo were on a papal mission, they maintained their usual trading activities. Everywhere they went there was commerce and bargaining, and much of Marco's narrative was written from a merchant's perspective. He mentioned that Tabriz had a large market for the pearls collected in the Persian Gulf, and he described the merchants' unusual practice of haggling over pearl prices. The bargaining was conducted silently, so onlookers could not find out how much money was exchanged: "the buyer and seller would squat opposite each other, throw a cloth over their hands, and then argue price and quality by pressure of the hidden fingers and wrists."[19]

From Iraq the Polos continued eastward across Persia, where they encountered a number of setbacks. Their caravan was assaulted by the Karaunas, a band of marauders who attacked the papal party and sold many of the Polos' companions into slavery. Marco, Niccolo, and Maffeo themselves narrowly escaped this fate. They continued overland to the port of Hormuz on the Persian Gulf, from which they had planned to sail to China. Upon

On their trek toward Persia, the Polos journeyed through the province of Mosul, known for its export of muslin.

horses were placed on top of cargo that had been covered with skins: "This makes it a risky undertaking to sail in these ships . . . because the Indian Ocean is often very stormy."[20] Because they believed it would be unsafe to sail from Hormuz, the Polos turned around and continued inland on a northeastern overland route, adding months to the journey.

Old Man of the Mountain

On the way back from Hormuz, the Polos encountered the region of Mulehet, which was the word for "heretics" in Arabic, and in one of his notebooks Marco recorded a story he heard. According to local history, a man known as the Old Man of the Mountain organized near Mulehet an army of men who were trained to kill at his request; he controlled this army by rewarding them with hashish, an intoxicating drug, and convincing them that they would go to paradise if

The Polos at the port of Hormuz, from which they planned to sail to China. Unsafe conditions at sea, however, forced the Polos to continue on an overland route.

arrival at Hormuz, however, they found the local ships to be unseaworthy. "Their ships are very bad," wrote Marco, "and many of them founder because they are not fastened with iron nails but stitched together with thread made of coconut husks." It was possible to lose cargo, he continued, because the vessels had no decks, and the

A manuscript detail depicts the Old Man of the Mountain giving orders to his followers. Marco described the Old Man and his fiercely loyal assassins in A Description of the World.

After leaving Mulehet, the Polos crossed the Pamir Mountains of Afghanistan, thought at the time to be the highest mountains in the world.

they died on a murderous mission. By playing with the soldiers' minds in this way, the Old Man of the Mountain built a capable and loyal army whose exploits were known throughout the Middle East. Marco Polo recorded the loyalty of these assassins to their lord in his book, *A Description of the World*, and some years later, a Florentine poet wrote that his devotion to love was "More than the Assassin to his Master or the Priest to God."[21] The story of these hired killers became entrenched in the European mind. In fact, the word *assassin*, which is derived from the word *hashish*, became the English term for "political murderer."

On the road from Mulehet, the Polos alternately crossed deserts and fertile areas as they climbed into the Pamir Mountains of Afghanistan. On the way, Marco, who enjoyed hunting and riding, found excellent game for his bow and arrow. But while the Polos were crossing a patch of the Persian desert, Marco contracted a fever that made him ill for months. Niccolo and Maffeo decided to wait in Badakhshan, Afghanistan, until the young man recovered completely.

Badakhshan was renowned for its healthy mountain climate, and Marco regained his health after doing some climbing, on the advice of the local people. While in the region of Badakhshan, Niccolo and Maffeo discovered vast ruby mines. But the regional monarch, who wanted to keep their value high, forbade their export, and the Polos were unable to trade for any of the gems.

With Marco in better health, the Polos resumed their crossing of the Pamirs, which were thought at that time to be the highest mountains in the world, and Marco noticed that the altitude there made it difficult to cook food or maintain fires. Marco also described the wild sheep who inhabit the mountains as having horns "from four to six palms in length."[22] The horns and bones of these animals were piled into high mounds along the mountain roads so that in deep snow travelers could follow the trails. Descending the Pamirs, the Polos trekked to the frontiers of the Gobi desert.

Strange Demons

What the local people told the Polos about the Gobi desert shocked them; it was rumored that the evil spirits who inhabited the desert sands "devise illusions to lead the unwary traveler to destruction if he lags behind or becomes separated from his companions."[23] Marco reported, "Often these voices make him stray from the path, so that he never finds it again . . . and in this way many travellers have been lost and have perished."[24] A Buddhist monk named Hsuan Tsang, who crossed the Gobi in A.D. 629, similarly recorded that he saw "all sorts of demon shapes and strange goblins, which seemed to surround him behind and before."[25]

The Polos were advised to tie bells to all their camels and pack animals so that they would be able to find each other again if they became separated. Before camping for the night, the Polos also set up a sign indicating the direction in which they were to continue traveling in the morning, so as not to become lost. Because winds covered their tracks with sand, and there was nothing but sand for miles in all directions, it was very easy to lose all sense of direction in the desert. After thirty days the Polo caravan finally had crossed the Gobi desert, and upon reaching the Chinese province of Kanchau, they decided to rest there for a few months and engage in commerce.

Marco became acquainted with the customs of Kanchau while his father and uncle traded in the city. He had learned to appraise merchandise and barter, too, but when he grew tired of trading he would go hunting on horseback or practice his falconry. Much of his time was also spent recording the customs and practices of the local people. Marco noted that the marriage customs of the people of Kanchau, like many of the Central Asian peoples, were very different from those of Europe. The men were polygamists, and took as many as thirty wives each, depending on their social status. It was common for a man to take his cousin as a wife or to

Trekking through the Pamir Mountains gave Marco ample opportunity to enjoy two of his passions—hunting and riding. This illustration from The Travels of Marco Polo *shows the Polos lion hunting.*

marry his brother's widow. Marco commented on these customs, saying, "Many things that we regard as grave sins are not sins at all in their eyes."[26] Marco understood a crucial point: social habits, customs, and traditions were not fixed, but varied in relation to where one lived. What seemed normal to a European might be considered bizarre by someone living in Asia, and vice versa. Though Marco may not have understood these marriage customs because they were so different from the traditions he had learned growing up in Europe, his experiences traveling in the Mongol Empire taught him to accept differences among peoples and even to appreciate them.

Eventually the Polos left Kanchau, and by the summer of 1275 they approached the vicinity of the Great Khan's palace, after a journey of three and a half years. By this time, the Polo family had traveled across numerous Asian plains, mountains, and deserts, and Marco had learned Turk-

ish and some Arabic and Mongol. The Polos were met on one of the empire's roads by a posse of messengers on horseback who had been dispatched by the khan. The Polos were surprised to learn that though they were still forty days' distance from the imperial city, the khan had heard news of their approach. The messengers informed them that this was because of the khan's postal and communication service, which had stations along the roads close enough together to permit an imperial messenger to travel 250 miles a day. By this method, which entailed exchanging horses five or six times, a messenger could make it from one end of the empire to another in a few weeks.

Arrival at Shang-tu

The khan's messengers escorted the Polos the rest of the way to his summer capital at

After three and a half years, the Polos finally reach their destination—the court of Kublai Khan.

The Polos before Kublai Khan. The Polos were warmly received and given luxurious accommodations at the khan's summer capital in Shang-tu.

Shang-tu, the walled city enclosing the khan's marble palace and pleasure park. Marco, who was fond of hunting and falconry, must have been impressed with the sixteen-mile hunting ground, for there were two hundred trained falcons living in the park, which contained all kinds of wild game, as well as tame leopards and cheetahs that helped the khan hunt.

Kublai welcomed the returning Polos, who prostrated themselves before him and then were received with great honor. Niccolo presented his son Marco, who was twenty-one, and the Great Khan was extremely pleased that the brothers had brought Marco with them. Marco graciously offered his services and allegiance to the fifty-nine-year-old khan, whom he described in this curious way:

The great lord of lords who is called Kublai is like this—he is of a fair size, neither short nor tall but of middle size. He is covered with flesh in a beautiful manner, not too fat or too lean; he is more than well formed in all parts. He has his face white and partly shining red like the color of a beautiful rose—the eyes black and beautiful, the nose very beautiful, well made and well set on the face.[27]

After a feast and reception honoring their return, the Polos gave the khan the letters from Gregory X and the holy oil and gifts the pope had sent. Kublai accommodated the Polos with luxurious apartments and made them comfortable, for he hoped they would stay and work at his court for a long time.

4 Khan-Balik: At the Court of the Great Khan

The Polos were soon introduced to daily life at the summer capital and, at summer's end, to life at the new official Mongol capital at Peking, China, which the Mongols had renamed Khan-balik, or City of the Great Khan. Today Khan-balik is known as Beijing, the capital of modern China. Kublai Khan had moved the Mongol capital to Peking in 1260, the year he announced a new era in Chinese history known as the Ta Yuan, or "Great Origin," dynasty. Living in Khan-balik and dining with the khan, the Polos soon learned the history of the Mongols and how they had come to control such a vast empire of conquered lands.

In 1206 Kublai's grandfather Genghis Khan had begun the Mongol Empire by campaigning in northern China, and by 1215 he had overthrown the reigning

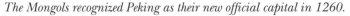

The Mongols recognized Peking as their new official capital in 1260.

Ch'in dynasty there. By 1222 Genghis had conquered much of the Middle East and had advanced his domains all the way to the border of Poland. His campaigns were carried on by his sons after his death, and his grandson Kublai came to the Mongol throne in 1256.

The Mongol Military

The Mongol army developed a reputation for barbarity and invincibility; according to one legend (which may have been invented to enlist European support against the Mongols), "to celebrate their victory in a befitting manner [the Mongol military] placed their victims under heavy planks, and, sitting on them, they feasted, exulting in their [enemies'] dying groans."[28] One of the factors behind the Mongols' military achievements was their skillful strategy, which included surprise attacks. In addition, the Mongols were adept at siege warfare and could starve a city to the point of defeat. The Mongols also used infantry and elephants in warfare.

Another factor in the success of the Mongol army was a technological advance in horsemanship known as the stirrup. The Mongol horsemen were among the first to put stirrups on their saddles, and it has been argued that the stirrup was actually a Mongol invention. Stirrups provided the Mongol horsemen with a more stable seat on their horses, which gave them greater mobility; with their feet planted firmly in stirrups, Mongol archers could pivot from side to side in their saddles and even shoot arrows behind their horses. Each soldier had several fast, hardy, Mongolian ponies at his disposal, so if one be-

The Mongols were among the first to attach stirrups to their saddles. This implement prevented the Mongols from floundering in the saddle. Rather, they were steady and lightning quick in battle.

came lame or was injured in battle, the cavalry trooper could continue to fight.

Khan-Balik, the Mongol Capital at Peking

Peking fell in 1215 to Genghis Khan, who partially destroyed the city, but Kublai Khan rebuilt Peking in 1260 when he moved the Mongol capital there and renamed the city "Khan-balik." Kublai built a city of twenty-five square miles around

The Khan's Concubines

Marco Polo's Description of the World *mentions that Kublai Khan employed only the most beautiful women in the empire as his sexual companions. This material is from Ronald Latham's translation of Marco's book.*

"After inspecting and surveying every girl feature by feature, her hair, her face, her eyebrows, her mouth, her lips, and every other feature, to see whether they are well-formed and in harmony with her person, the valuers award to some girls a score of sixteen marks, to others seventeen, eighteen, or twenty, or more or less according to the degree of their beauty . . . the thirty or forty with the highest score are selected for [the khan's] chamber. These are first allotted, one by one, to the barons' wives, who are instructed to observe them carefully at night in their chambers, to make sure that they are virgins and not blemished or defective in any member, that they sleep sweetly without snoring, and that their breath is sweet and they give out no unpleasant odor. Then those who are approved are divided into groups of six, who serve the Khan for three days and three nights at a time in his chamber and his bed, ministering to all his needs. And he uses them according to his pleasure. After three days and three nights, in come the next six damsels. And so they continue in rotation throughout the year.

While some of the group are in attendance in their lord's chamber, the others are waiting in an ante-chamber near by. If he is in need of anything from outside, such as food or drink, the damsels inside the chamber pass word to those outside, who immediately get it ready. In this way the Khan is served by no one except these damsels. As for the other damsels, who are rated at a lower score, they remain with the Khan's other women in the palace, where they are instructed in needle-work, glove-making, and other elegant accomplishments. When some nobleman is looking for a wife, the Great Khan gives him one of these damsels with a great dowry. And in this way he marries them all off honorably."

the existing urban area and laid out the streets in geometric patterns, which Marco described: "From one side to the other of the town [the streets] are drawn out straight as a thread, and in this way all the city inside is laid out by squares, as a chessboard is."[29] Khan-balik was a city of walls; it was divided into three concentric squares, each surrounded by a packed earthen or brick wall twelve to eighteen feet high. These squares were known as the imperial city, the Tatar city, and the outer city. Each square of the city had eight gates, and the outer square had watchtowers along all the gates, out of which led roadways to various parts of the empire. Suburbs outside the city contained even more people than the walled city of Khan-balik itself.

The outer square of the city was inhabited by merchants, tradesmen, and citizens. There were also quarters for the city's vast population of prostitutes, who were employed by Kublai's court to serve visiting heads of state. The next square of the city, between the outer square and the inner square, was known as the Tatar city because it was home to the khan's bodyguards and soldiers, who hailed from all parts of the empire. In the innermost section of Khan-balik, the imperial city, were the khan's palace and personal apartments, as well as the living quarters of the other members of Kublai's court: concubines, eunuchs, servants, and the royal family.

In the outermost city all activity was regulated by the Bell Tower, a monument Kublai constructed in his palace park from which a bell tolled three times each evening, signaling the close of the day. "Once this bell has sounded the due number of peals," Marco wrote, "no one ventures abroad in the city except in cases of childbirth or illness, and those who are called out by such emergencies are obliged to carry lights."[30] No one in the outer city was allowed to keep a light on indoors after the nightly tolling of the bell, either. By making it virtually illegal to hold secret meetings at night, these regulations helped to discourage people from plotting revolt or insurrection. The Bell Tower constructed by Kublai in 1272 is one of the few surviving examples of the Mongol occupation in the city of Beijing today.

The innermost section of Khan-balik housed the palace of Kublai Khan, where members of the royal family and others lived.

The Mongol government levied taxes on the people of the empire that were collected by the various khans and barons, and the central government also hoarded all metal coins and passed out notes of currency on paper, a practice adopted from the deposed Chinese emperor. Paper currency was a new idea at the time and had not yet been introduced to Europe, so Marco was impressed by it. Printing paper money was a way for a ruler to accumulate great stores of wealth, for while other people used paper money instead of gold to pay for things, the ruler collected all the gold that formerly was used as currency. Marco noted one of the greatest advantages of paper money when he commented, "And I can tell you that the papers that reckon as ten gold bezants do not weigh one."[31]

The Chinese system of government was adopted by the Mongols as their own, but the Chinese were not allowed to serve in the Mongol government because it was feared they might plot a rebellion. The only Chinese people allowed at the khan's court were servants and those skilled in painting or astrology. Because the Mongol Empire required a great number of civil servants for its administration, Kublai Khan was always looking for educated foreigners like the Polos to employ in this capacity. The Polos were probably the only Europeans ever employed at Kublai's court. Most government workers were Mongols, or foreigners from western Asia.

Though the empire was divided into khanates ruled by lesser khans loyal to the Great Khan, twelve barons also supervised the Mongol government and were in charge of the empire's thirty-four provinces. Each had his own palace, which housed a judge and a staff of clerks. Twelve more barons were also employed to supervise the military. The social position the Polos occupied at Kublai's court was similar to that of these barons, and they enjoyed the same privileges of dining with the khan and being present at all official and ceremonial functions.

From Marco Polo's descriptions we have an idea of what a feast was like in the

Kublai Khan had such respect and admiration for the Polos that he employed them as government workers. Here the Polos levy taxes for salt, spice, and wine.

Kublai Khan and the Polos travel in an ornate coach carried on the backs of elephants. This is just one example of the luxurious life led by those close to the khan.

khan's dining room. Silver trumpets announced Kublai's entry to guests, who bowed at his passing. Every time the khan raised his goblet to drink, court musicians played a burst of music and all the company bowed low as Kublai quaffed his wine. The waiters wore silk handkerchiefs tied over the mouth and nose so that the food would not be touched by their breath. When the Great Khan held court or planned a wedding, the feasts were enormous. Marco described the seating arrangements for such occasions, which reflect the class distinctions present at the court:

> [Kublai Khan] sits himself at a much higher table than the rest at the northern end of the hall, so that he faces south. His principal wife sits next to him on the left. On the right, at a somewhat lower level, sit his sons in order of age . . . and his grandsons and kinsmen of imperial lineage. They are placed so their heads are on a level with the Great Khan's feet. Next to them are seated the other noblemen at other tables lower down again. . . . All the wives of the Khan's sons and grandsons and kinsmen are seated on his left at a lower level, and next to them the wives of his nobles and knights lower down still. And they all know their appointed place in the lord's plan. But you must not imagine that all the guests sit at tables; for most of the knights and nobles in the hall take their meal seated on carpets for want of tables.[32]

After such a feast, the guests were treated to entertainment provided by jugglers, acrobats, or magicians, and they could walk in the khan's gardens, including the wooded park known as Pei Hai, in which Kublai had transplanted a certain blue flower native to the Mongolian steppes which reminded him of his ancestors.

While Kublai held court and hosted celebratory feasts, others were not so fortunate. During the Polos' stay at Khan-balik, a Chinese general also lived there, held captive in a dungeon so that he could not organize an insurrection against Mongol rule in China. The general's despair over his imprisonment and China's subjection to foreign rule contrasts sharply with the luxurious life led at court by the Mongol conquerors.

> My dungeon is lighted by the will-o-the-wisp alone; No breath of spring cheers the murky solitude in which I dwell. Exposed to mist and dew, I had many times thought to die; and yet, through the seasons of two revolving years, disease hovered around me in vain. The dank, unhealthy soil to me became Paradise itself. For there was that within me which misfortune could not steal away; and so I remained firm, gazing at the white clouds floating over my head, and bearing in my heart a sorrow boundless as the sky.[33]

The Chinese people resented being ruled by the Mongols, and they objected to the sight of the khan's soldiers on the streets. Kublai Khan was the first foreigner in history to conquer all of China, and when he established the Mongol capital at Peking, he removed the captive Chinese emperor and his wife and put them in a retirement palace, where they were allowed to remain unharmed. The entire Chinese government administration was exiled. Many of the Chinese intellectuals and civil servants who had been deprived of their places at court and in the government awaited an opportunity to overthrow the Mongol yoke. When renowned Chinese painters and astrologers were called to do work for the Great Khan, many re-

fused and accepted punishment rather than submit to the khan's orders.

Marco Becomes Messenger for the Khan

Marco quickly mastered the writing systems of the four languages he had learned to speak—Mongol, Turkish, Persian, and Arabic. In 1277, two years after his arrival at the khan's court, Marco was nominated as commissioner to the imperial council, a position similar to that of an overseer, and in this capacity he went on many diplomatic missions around the empire. In exchange for his loyalty to the khan, Marco was fed, clothed, sheltered, and protected by the emperor, who also gave him many costly gifts. Kublai was glad to be able to use Marco as a messenger, for he trusted Marco not to lie to him about the state of affairs in the empire, and because he liked the way the young man related stories he had heard and described the customs and traditions he had observed on his travels in the empire. Knowing that Marco had a knack for remembering such cultural details, Kublai wanted to send the young Venetian on missions around the empire—not only for diplomatic or political reasons, but so that Marco, on returning, could entertain the khan with tales of the strange and curious things he had observed. Kublai detested messengers who returned from distant places with nothing to tell, but Marco always made notes in little books, and sometimes he even brought back curios for the khan. These notes and objects were the kind of information Kublai really wanted from his emissaries; he wanted to hear how other people lived,

Chinese Funeral Customs

While staying in Fu-Chau, China, Marco Polo recorded the local funeral customs, which differed tremendously from anything he had ever seen. This excerpt is from Ronald Latham's translation of The Travels.

"When the deceased is being carried from his house to the place where he is to be cremated, at some point on the route his kinsfolk have erected in the middle of the road a wooden house draped with silk and cloth of gold. On arriving in front of this house, the cortege [procession] halts; and the mourners fling down wine and food in plenty before the dead. This they do because they say that he will be received with like honor in the next world. When he is brought to the place where he is to be cremated, his kindred provide images cut out of paper representing horses and camels and pieces of money, and all this they burn with the body. And they say that in the next world the dead will have as many slaves and beasts and coins as the paper images that are burnt.

While the body remains unburnt in the house, they preserve it in this manner: they take a coffin of boards of the thickness of a palm firmly joined together and all splendidly painted, and put the body inside, embalmed with camphor and other spices. Then they stop the chinks in the coffin with pitch and lime, so that it does not cause a stench in the house, and cover it with silken shrouds. So long as the body remains in the house, the inhabitants of the house lay a table every day for the deceased and serve food and drink for him just as if he were alive; they set it in front of the coffin and leave it long enough to be eaten, and say that the soul has eaten some of this food. This is how they keep it until the day when they take it away for cremation. . . . All this they do for fear of offending the spirits of the dead."

what gods they believed in, what games they played, and all kinds of information of that sort. As one edition of Marco's *Description of the World* says:

Marco was in the Great Khan's court XVII years, and when any great embassage or business should be done in any of his countries or provinces, he was always sent, wherefor, diverse great men of the Court did envy him, but always kept this order, that whatever he saw or heard, were it good or evil, he always wrote it, and had it in mind to declare to the Great Khan in order.[34]

Kublai preferred Marco over all his other messengers, and he enjoyed Marco's company more than that of his barons. Unsurprisingly, many of the barons became jealous of this overt favoritism. The khan grew to rely on Marco as a messenger and on the views of the elder Polos, whose opinion he valued and whom he occasionally consulted on military affairs. Marco's book mentions that when the khan asked the Polo brothers about European warfare technology, Niccolo and Maffeo constructed a wooden artillery machine like those used for siege warfare in Europe, which could hurl three-hundred-pound stones at the enemy.

Missions for the Khan

Kublai sent Marco on numerous trips around the empire, and Marco never disappointed him by coming back with nothing to report. Marco's book shows him to have been a keen observer of folklore and ethnographic details. On his first imperial mission Marco was sent to the borders of Tibet and the Chinese province of Yunnan, a remote region which the Mongolian administration had trouble supervising. Marco was to inspect the situation there and let Kublai Khan know what was happening, but the khan also expected Marco to tell him how the people lived.

While traveling in Tibet, Marco uncovered some marital customs that differed widely from those he had known. Whereas in Europe, virginity was a quality coveted in a bride, the most highly esteemed

Marco Polo on an expedition for the khan. Kublai relied on Marco to bring him accurate, entertaining accounts of the peoples and customs he observed on his travels.

women in one region of Tibet were those who had had the most lovers. Indeed, the mothers in the villages offered their daughters to male travelers, with the idea that the men would give out trinkets to show that they had slept with the young women. These trinkets were worn on necklaces, and, Marco recorded, "she that has the most tokens is the most highly esteemed as a wife; for they say that she is the most favored by the gods."[35]

While Marco was in Yunnan he saw crocodiles for the first time. Calling the reptiles "beasts," he described them to Kublai:

There are some of them ten paces in length that are as thick as a stout cask, for their girth runs to about ten palms. . . . They have two squat legs in front near the head, which have no feet but simply three claws, two small and one bigger, like the claws of a lion or falcon. They have enormous heads and eyes so bulging that they are bigger than loaves. Their mouth is big enough to swallow a man at one gulp. Their teeth are huge.[36]

On another journey for the Great Khan, Marco was sent to Burma, which lies just east of India. There he observed people practicing the art of tattooing. "All the people alike, male or female . . . have their flesh covered all over with pictures of lions and dragons and birds and other objects, made with needles in such a way as they are indelible."[37] Marco also noticed that tattoos were worn as a sign of high social status and to impart sexual appeal, but he adds that during the process of being tattooed, "the victim suffers what might well pass for the pains of Purgatory," as he or she was tied down and pricked with as many as five needles at once and then subjected to having ink rubbed into the wounds.

Marco compiled these descriptions of life in various regions of the Mongol Empire for Kublai Khan and ultimately published them in his own book. They represent a vast resource of information for modern ethnologists and anthropologists, who are able to know something of the customs of these regions during the Middle Ages. Historian Leonardo Olschki, in describing Marco's book, said "this vast assemblage of data, brief mentions, and reminiscences is collected within the plan of Marco's itineraries, which led to the discovery of a world that was either completely unknown or had been distorted for

After a trip to India, the Polos present trinkets to the khan.

An illustration of Marco's account of pearl fishing off the coast of southern India. India is just one of the many regions he observed during his travels for the khan.

centuries by traditional fables."[38] Information on Asian history, medicine, plant and animal life, and folklore that might never have been available to Europeans in Marco Polo's time became known because of Marco's informal research.

Despite their many journeys for the khan, Marco and his father and uncle (who occasionally accompanied Marco on his trips) began to think of faraway Venice and how they would return there. The Polos were shrewd men, and they knew that as Kublai grew older their chances for leaving the empire safely decreased, for travel always became difficult when a ruler died. Though they stayed with Kublai for seventeen years, the Polos could not help but think of their eventual departure.

5 Escape from Khan-Balik

Disillusionment

Slowly and sadly
The River flows
On its long journey
To the sea.
A solitary wild goose
Calls under the moon,
And the night
Is agleam with frost

. . . . .

If for ten long years
You have wandered
In the distant lands
Of the earth
Be not in too much haste
To seek
News of your faraway home.
—Wang Tso[39]

During their seventeen-year stay at Kublai Khan's court, the Polos often thought of their home and family in Venice. But by 1290 returning seemed especially important, for the Polos feared that if they did not leave soon, they might never get out. Kublai Khan was seventy-five years old, and he was growing feebler each year. His empire was waning, and he no longer exercised the same control he had once wielded. The Polos had made a fortune for themselves under his administration, but they had also acquired enemies who were jealous of the favor the khan showed them. If the Polos were still in the Mongol Empire when the Khan died, they would no longer be protected, and not only their wealth but also their lives would be in jeopardy. The Polos feared that the khan's death could mean the end of law and order in the empire; news of his demise might spark rebellions, and then it would be impossible to travel safely on the caravan routes.

The Polos knew from experience that the period between one monarch's death and the accession of a new ruling power was a volatile interval during which anything might happen. If the Chinese attempted to recover the throne, all allies of the Mongol Empire would be killed. Or, a rival faction in the khan's own court might try to put a man in power. In 1340, a guide for would-be travelers to China warned of the consequences of the death of a ruler:

When the lord dies, and until the other lord who should rule is proclaimed, in this interim sometimes irregular acts have been done to the Franks and to other foreigners. . . . And the road will not be safe until the other lord who is to reign in the place of him who is dead is proclaimed.[40]

Several times the Polos asked the khan for permission to leave, but each time the khan refused, because "he was so fond of them and so much enjoyed their company that nothing would induce him to give them leave."[41] Kublai had grown very attached to the Polos. On another occasion Niccolo tried to persuade the khan to let them leave:

> Messer Niccolo one day, seeing the Great Khan in high good humour, seized the occasion, and, on bended knee begged him, in the name of all three, for permission to depart. At these words [the khan] was much disturbed. And he spoke to him, asking him what reason moved him to desire to set out on such a long and perilous journey, during which they could all easily die. And if it were because of wealth or of anything else, he would gladly give them the double of what they had at their home, and heap upon them as many honors as they might desire. And, for the great love which he bore them, he refused them flatly the right to depart.[42]

A Chance to Escape

With the patience of those who had traveled for many years in the Middle East and Asia, often being delayed for long periods of time by war or inclement weather, the Polos bided their time until an opportunity for leaving the empire might present itself. That opportunity came in the form of three ambassadors from the court of Arghun, the khan of Persia, who arrived in Khan-balik around 1292. Bulagan, the wife of the Persian khan, had died and

left a will requesting that her husband's next wife be of her lineage. Therefore Arghun dispatched envoys to Kublai Khan's court asking him to select a new wife for him from Bulagan's relatives. Kublai, who was Arghun's great-uncle, selected a beautiful seventeen-year-old girl named Kokachin to become Arghun Khan's new bride.

The Persian envoys departed with Kokachin and her retinue of servants, but soon they were forced to turn back to Khan-balik because tribal wars had blocked the overland caravan routes. The Persian ambassadors decided they would prefer to undertake a sea voyage rather than wait for the land routes to become passable. While Kokachin's escorts were still at Khan-balik, Marco Polo returned by sea from an imperial mission to India with many stories about his journey. The

A portrait of Marco Polo during his older years. Polo spent seventeen years in Khan-balik.

Kublai Khan adamantly refused to grant the Polos permission to leave his empire.

three Persian ambassadors became interested in Marco Polo because of his knowledge of parts of the sea route to Persia. Quickly seizing what they saw as their ticket to Venice, the Polos offered to escort Arghun Khan's ambassadors and Princess Kokachin on a sea voyage to Persia.

To persuade Kublai Khan to let them go, the Polos pointed out that their presence on the mission would show the Persian khan that he was being highly honored by the Mongol emperor, for the Polos, with their knowledge of sailing the southeastern seas, could ensure that the party would arrive safely in Persia. The Persian ambassadors also asked Kublai if the Polos could accompany them on their journey. Kublai Khan was reluctant to let the Polos go, but, perhaps because he did not want to affront the Persian khan, who was a powerful ruler, he agreed to their departure.

Preparing for a Sea Voyage

In preparation for their journey home, the Polos exchanged all the possessions they had acquired over their seventeen-year stay in Khan-balik for small, transportable items of value: jewels, spices, incense, and cloth. As a special precaution due to the dangers of traveling, the Polos sewed their jewels into the linings and seams of their clothing; this would guard against loss if the ship were overtaken by pirates or if, later in their journey, their caravan were attacked by pirates or bandits. The Polos also may have chosen this form of concealment because the export of jewels was forbidden.

Meanwhile, Kublai Khan had outfitted a fleet of fourteen ships, each with four

Tales of Island Cannibals

While sailing for Persia with Princess Kokachin, the Polos were forced to wait for five months on Sumatra until the weather improved and they could sail again. Ronald Latham's translation of The Travels *records that some of the native islanders practiced cannibalism.*

"You must know that, when one of them, male or female, falls sick, the kinsfolk send for the magicians to find out whether the patient is due to recover. And these magicians claim by means of their enchantments and their idols and diabolic art to know whether he is destined to recover or to die. You must not suppose, because I speak of 'diabolic art,' that that is their account of the matter: they attribute their knowledge to the power of the gods working through a medium of their art. If they say that he is due to die, then the kinsfolk send for certain men who are specially appointed to put such persons to death. These men come and seize the patient and put something over his mouth so as to suffocate him. When he is dead, they cook him. Then all his kinsfolk assemble and eat him whole.

I assure you that they even devour all the marrow in his bones. This they do because they do not want one scrap of his substance to remain. For they say that if any scrap remained then this substance would generate worms, which would thereupon die for want of food. And by the death of these worms they declare the dead man's soul would incur great sin and torment, because so many souls generated by his substance met their deaths. That is why they eat him whole. After they have eaten him, they take his bones and put them in a handsome casket. Then they carry this and hang it in a huge cavern in the mountains, in some place where no beast or other evil thing can touch it."

masts and as many as twelve sails, for the three ambassadors, Princess Kokachin and her attendants, the Polos, the crew of sailors, and the serving people. The expedition also included the daughter of the king of Manzi, whom Kublai had decided to send to Arghun Khan as well, an indication of Kublai's desire to please the Persian ruler.

According to Marco's own account, four of the ships prepared for the expedition carried crews of as many as 250 sailors. The ships were stocked with enough provisions to last two years. The

Arghun Khan in his garden in Persia. When Kokachin was selected to be Arghun's bride, the Polos offered to escort the princess to Persia.

vessels were built of fir and pine, and Marco's description of them includes the earliest mention of watertight compartments in shipbuilding, an invention unknown in Europe until much later:

Some of the ships, that is the bigger ones, have also thirteen bulkheads or partitions made of stout planks dovetailed into one another. This is useful in case the ship's hull should chance to be damaged in some place by striking on a reef or being rammed by a whale in search of food—a not infrequent occurrence, for if a whale happens to pass near the ship while she is sailing at night and churning the water to foam, he may infer from the white gleam in the water that there is food for him there and so charge full tilt against the ship and ram her, often breaching the hull at some point. In that event the water coming through the breach will run into the bilge, which is never permanently occupied. The sailors promptly find out where the breach is. Cargo is shifted from the damaged compartment into the neighboring ones; for the bulkheads are so stoutly built that the compartments are watertight. The damage is then repaired and the cargo shifted back.[43]

Kublai Khan outfitted a fleet of fourteen ships for the Polos' journey to Arghun's home. Marco's description of these vessels included the earliest mention of watertight compartments in shipbuilding.

Before their departure, Kublai Khan gives the Polos golden tablets that guaranteed their safe travel in the Mongol Empire.

Just before their departure, Kublai Khan brought the Polos before him and gave them two tablets that guaranteed their safe travel in his empire. He also gave them personal messages for the pope, the kings of France, Spain, and England, and some other Christian rulers. Once again the Polos were entrusted to act as the khan's ambassadors to foreign heads of state.

The Polos Leave Khan-Balik

In 1292 the party set sail from the coast of Ch'uan-chou, in southern China. They sailed for three months, passing the southern tip of Singapore and sailing through the Malacca straits by Sumatra, where Marco Polo's book records that the expedition landed in the kingdom of Sumatra

A fanciful illustration shows a seaman blasting farewell as the Polos embark on their journey home.

Mind over Matter: The Hindu Yogis of India

While traveling along India's Malabar coast, the Polos observed Hindu holy men, who fasted, lived for more than a century, and cared for the well being of all living creatures, even worms. These customs are mentioned in Ronald Latham's translation of Marco's Description of the World.

"There is a regular religious order in this kingdom of Malabar, of those who are called by this name of Yogi, who carry abstinence to the extremes of which I will tell you and lead a harsh and austere life. . . . They live even longer than the others, as much as 150 or 200 years. And their bodies remain so active that they can still come and go as they will and perform all the services required by their monastery and their idols and serve them just as well as if they were younger. This comes of their great abstinence and of eating very little food and only what is wholesome. For it is their practice to eat chiefly rice and milk. . . .

They take their food on the leaves of apples of paradise or other big leaves—not green leaves, but dried ones; for they say that the green leaves have souls, so that this would be a sin. For in their dealings with all living creatures they are at pains to do nothing that they believe to be a sin. Indeed they would sooner die than do anything that they deemed to be sinful. . . .

When they wish to relieve their bowels, they go to the beach of the sea-shore and there void their excrement in the sand by the water. Then, after cleansing themselves in the water, they take a stick with which they spread out their excrement and so crumble it into the sand that nothing is visible. When asked why they do this, they reply: 'This would breed worms. And the worms thus created, when their food was consumed by the sun, would starve to death. And since that substance issues from our bodies—for without food we cannot live—we should incur grievous sin by the death of so many souls created of our substance. Therefore we annihilate this substance, so that no worms may be created from it merely to die of starvation by our guilt and default.'"

(which was not then the name of the whole island). There they waited in a fort for five months until the weather improved enough to allow them to continue—probably, that is, until the monsoon season had passed. They built the fort as protection against people in the region, whom they had heard were cannibals. As it happened, however, they had no trouble from the Sumatrans and even traded with them for rice and palm wine.

While in Sumatra Marco Polo wrote of a variety of animals he had never seen or heard of before; he mistook orangutans (which are only found on the islands of Sumatra and Borneo) for people and described them as human beings: "I give you my word that in this kingdom there are men who have tails fully a palm in length. They are not at all hairy. This is true of most of the men—that is, of those who live outside in the mountains, not of those in the city. Their tails are as thick as a dog's."[44] Marco's misjudgment reveals how easy it is for people from different cultures to fail to understand one another because of dissimilarities in appearance.

Marco also observed rhinoceroses on Sumatra and thought they must be unicorns, though he admitted that they looked nothing at all like European depictions of unicorns.

When the winds had changed to a favorable direction, the expedition left Sumatra and sailed to the northern coast of the island of Ceylon, which is now called Sri Lanka. In Ceylon Marco observed the largest ruby he had ever seen. "It is about a palm in length and the thickness of a man's arm."[45] The gem, which belonged to the king of Ceylon, who had inherited it from his ancestors, may have been the same ruby mentioned in the diary of Hsuan Tsang, who had visited Ceylon six centuries before Marco Polo. The Chinese monk recorded that a ruby atop Ceylon's most sacred pagoda was so large that it resembled a flashing star at night. Marco's book tells us that Kublai Khan had heard of this ruby and had sent emissaries to the king of Ceylon asking to buy it, but the king had replied that the ruby was not for sale at any price. In Ceylon Marco also heard the story of the Buddha

During their travels, the Polos encountered many exotic animals. In his writings, Marco described these strange beasts.

and how he became a god. With remarkable religious tolerance for a thirteenth-century Catholic, Marco said the Buddha sounded like a most austere and virtuous man, and that "had he been a Christian, he would have been a great saint with our Lord Jesus Christ."[46]

"To Sit on the Earth Is Honorable Enough"

From Ceylon the expedition sailed around the tip of India, and along the western coast of the subcontinent, docking at several points along the way. In India Marco recorded a number of Hindu customs that continue to be practiced there today. "The people of this kingdom [India] worship idols. Most of them worship the ox, because they say that it is a very good thing. No one would eat beef for anything in the world, and no one would kill an ox on any account."[47] Marco went on to describe the customs of those referred to as yogis:

They worship the ox and most of them carry a little ox made of gilt copper or bronze in the middle of the forehead . . . they burn cow-dung and make a powder of it. With this they anoint various parts of their body with great reverence, no less than Christians display in the use of holy water. . . . I assure you further that they would not kill any creature or any living thing in the world, neither fly nor flea nor louse nor any other vermin, because they say that they have souls. For the same reason they refuse to eat living things because of the sin they would incur . . . they do not eat anything fresh, either herb or root, until it is dried; be-

cause they declare that while they are fresh they have souls.[48]

Marco also revealed a glimmer of comprehension of the religious worldview of the Indian people:

The king and his barons and everyone else all sit on the earth. If you ask them why they do not seat themselves more honorably, they reply that to sit on the earth is honorable enough, because we are made from the earth and to the earth we must return, so that no one could honor the earth too highly and no one should slight it.[49]

On the Malabar coast of India, Marco visited a region known as Motupalli, in which diamonds were harvested from the area's mountain gorges and caverns. The gorges were too steep to navigate, and the diamonds could not be reached by human hands, so the people devised other methods of retrieving the gems from the floor of the gorges.

They take many lumps of flesh imbued [soaked] in blood and fling them down into the depths of the valley. And the lumps thus flung down pick up great numbers of diamonds, which become embedded in the flesh. Now it so happens that these mountains are inhabited by a great many white eagles . . . when these eagles spy the flesh lying at the bottom of the valley, down they swoop and seize the lumps and carry them off. The men observe attentively where the eagles go, and as soon as they see that a bird has alighted and is swallowing the flesh, they rush to the spot as fast as they can. Scared by their sudden approach, the eagles fly away, leaving the flesh behind

Arghun Khan died during the Polos two-year voyage to Hormuz, Persia. Kokachin then married Arghun's son Ghazan.

with plenty of diamonds embedded in it. Another means by which they get the diamonds is this. When the eagles eat the flesh, they also eat—that is, they swallow—the diamonds. [The eagle] deposits the diamonds it has swallowed with its droppings. So men come and collect these droppings, and there too they find diamonds in plenty.[50]

From the Arabian Sea the Polos and their expedition finally approached Persia and the Gulf of Oman. By this time many of their passengers, including two of the Persian ambassadors, had died, presumably of some epidemic, but Princess Kokachin was still alive and well. Marco does not mention what happened to the daughter of the king of Manzi. When their expedition arrived in Hormuz, Persia, two years after departing from China, the Polos and the surviving Persian ambassador

discovered that Arghun Khan had died. He had been temporarily replaced as khan of Persia by his brother Kaikhatu, who accepted the princess Kokachin as a wife for Arghun's son Ghazan, the rightful heir, who was then with the army at Persia's border fighting off enemy raids.

Kaikhatu presented the Polos with gold tablets similar to those Kublai Khan had given them, inscribed with the order that the Polos be treated as Kaikhatu himself. In addition, they were given horses, food, and protection for the rest of their journey through Persia. The princess Kokachin wept when the Polos left. She had come to regard the Venetians as her fathers, and they had treated her as their own daughter, protecting her throughout the long journey with great honor.

Having left the royal retinue behind in Persia, the Polos and their personal servants continued in a small caravan overland through Persia, where they often used Kaikhatu's passports to obtain an escort of as many as two hundred men on horseback through some of the most dangerous sections of the country. Such a large escort was often necessary for protection, as the entire region was in upheaval following the death of Arghun Khan.

The Polos trekked overland, backtracking much the same route they had taken on the way to Hormuz more than two decades earlier. From Hormuz they traveled on camels to Trebizond, a Greek colony on the Black Sea, which bordered the Mongol Empire. The old Latin empire

During his many travels, Polo picked up the customs and attitudes of many different cultures. Here, Polo is dressed in the fashion of the Tatars.

of the crusaders had been overthrown years before by the Greeks, with help from Venice's rivals, the Genoese, so now the Genoese, not the Venetians, enjoyed trade privileges in Trebizond, Constantinople, and other Greek ports. It is unlikely that the Polos on their arrival, had any idea of the political climate in Trebizond or of how much the Genoese-Venetian rivalry had grown during their absence, for they seem to have assumed that it was safe for Venetians to travel there. When some Greek subjects in Trebizond discovered that the Polos were Venetian, however, they robbed them of many possessions. The Venetian republic was informed of this trespass against the Polos and even intervened on the Polos' behalf, but the travelers were never compensated fully for their losses.

From Trebizond, the Polos sailed across the Black Sea to Constantinople, where they also found that they were no longer as welcome as they had been before the Greeks reclaimed the city from the Latin crusaders. From Constantinople they sailed to Negroponte in Greece and finally to Venice, where they arrived in 1295, having traveled nearly fifteen-thousand miles since leaving Europe twenty-four years earlier.

Kublai Khan, the Great Khan of the Mongols, died before the Polos reached Venice. It is not known whether the Polos were aware of the khan's death, but they could not have been surprised, since anticipation of this event had prompted them to leave Khan-balik in the first place. The Polos were fortunate to be in Europe, away from the chaos that accompanied the death of a ruler, especially a ruler of such an immense empire. As Marco said to his father Niccolo, "It must be God's pleasure that we return to Venice to tell people of all the things the world contains."[51]

6 Back in Venice

The Polos must have looked like foreigners when they returned to Venice, for their skin had turned dark and leathery, like that of long-time travelers in arid lands. One historian attempted to explain their appearance. "They had an indescribable something of the Tartar in their aspect and in their way of speech, having almost forgotten the Venetian tongue. Those garments of theirs were much the worse for wear, and were made of coarse cloth, and cut after the fashion of the Tartars."[52]

Marco, Maffeo, and Niccolo on their return to Venice. The trio had been gone so long that they were not recognized by their fellow Venetians.

In any event Maffeo, Niccolo, and Marco were not recognized and had to force their way into their own home. Only by displaying their accumulated wealth of jewels, incense, cloth, and other Eastern wares did the Polos succeed in proving their identity to relatives who had believed them to be dead. The news of their return, with fabulous wealth, quickly spread through Venice, and according to Giambattista Ramusio, a sixteenth-century biographer of Marco Polo, "the whole city, gentry as well as common folk, flocked to their house, to embrace them and to shower them with caresses and demonstrations of affection and reverence, as great as you can possibly imagine."[53]

The Polos Suffer Culture Shock

Adjusting to life in Venice after traveling for so many years in lands where customs, manners, and morals were markedly different must have been difficult for Marco, Maffeo, and Niccolo. Surely their return to Europe produced culture shock on an immense scale. Especially difficult was convincing others of what they had seen and experienced in Asia; whenever Marco described life in the Mongol capital or told stories of his travels, people listened in fascination, but they refused to believe that such tales could be true. The Venetians liked to listen to his stories because they seemed so exotic, but they liked to laugh about them afterward, too, and they remained skeptical about what they had heard. Marco's description of the world was so different from their own experience that it was beyond the reach of their imagination. Marco might show visitors items he had brought back from the East—yak hair, sago flour, or musk—but it was impossible to make people accept the accompanying stories.

Nevertheless, Marco, even at forty-one, was a versatile man, used to adapting to different situations, and he adjusted to the change from being a globe-trotter to leading a sedentary life as a well-to-do bachelor and merchant in Venice. Marco still had a lot to learn about the merchant trade. Commerce was handled differently in the West and in the East, so he had to forget Eastern values and units of currency, as well as his years of experience in silent, tactile bargaining, and learn cur-

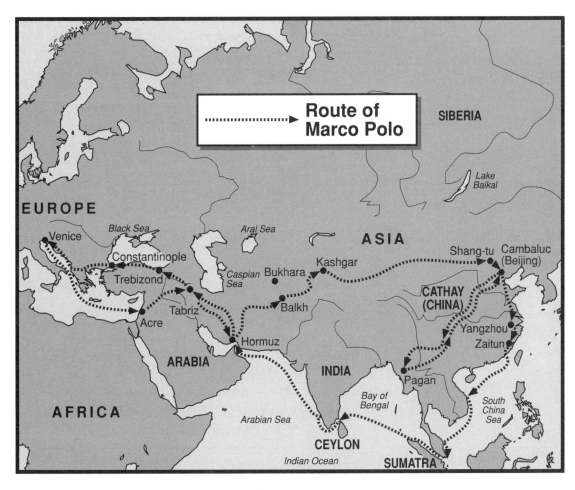

A Failed Revolution

On St. Vito's day in 1310, Bajamonte Tiepolo launched a conspiracy to assassinate the leaders of the Venetian republic and the doge of Venice, its chief magistrate. Historian Henry Hart records in Marco Polo: Venetian Adventurer *that as Tiepolo's insurrectionists gathered in the streets of the city, it was stopped by the act of one Venetian woman.*

"As Tiepolo with his contingent marched shouting and brandishing their weapons down the Merceria, the householders, loving a brawl, began to attack them from all sides, pelting them with stones and any missiles that came to hand. . . . A certain woman, Giustina Rosso, hearing the blood-curdling cry, 'Death to tyranny!' under her window, threw open the casement and looked down upon the crowd, an action strictly forbidden by Venetian law. Taking in the situation at a glance she thought not at all of the law but seized a great stone mortar filled with growing red carnations and flung it with all her force at the head of Bajamonte Tiepolo. The heavy missile missed the leader, but struck the head of his standard bearer. He fell, and Tiepolo was spattered with his blood and brains. This unforeseen disaster struck terror into Tiepolo's men, for they were jammed tightly in the narrow street between high walls, and missiles were now raining down on them mercilessly from window and rooftop. Terror grew to panic, and the conspirators turned and fled to the wooden bridge of the Rialto, where Tiepolo was finally persuaded to lay down his arms. . . .

In due time Giustina Rosso was summoned before the Doge to receive the thanks of the grateful Republic. Being asked to name her own reward for her brave deed, she modestly refused recompense but finally admitted that she would like permission to hang out of her window a banner of San Marco [St. Mark, the patron saint of Venice] each St. Vito's Day, and moreover asked that her rent never be raised above fifteen gold ducats a year. The story went the round of all the canals and squares, and the house was pointed out to all as the Casa Giustina, whose tenant would take no recompense from the Doge for her brave act."

rent Western values of merchandise. One major adjustment for Marco, Niccolo, and Maffeo was learning to accept Venice's diminished influence at the trading ports on the Black Sea and on the Mediterranean. The Polos had left Venice in 1271, at the height of its power and influence, returning home when Venice cast a mere shadow of its former glory, poorer now than its rival city-state, Genoa, which had the upper hand in sea trade.

The rivalry between Genoa and Venice had escalated in the 1290s, as the two city-states competed for the Levantine trade. In 1291, when the Muslims recaptured the Mediterranean port of Acre from the Latin crusaders, the Venetians received from the Muslims exclusive rights to escort pilgrims to Acre, an arrangement that gave Venice a trading advantage over Genoa in the Muslim city. The Genoese retaliated by asking the Greek emperor to prohibit Venetians from trading in the lands bordering the Aegean Sea. These attempts to hurt each other's trade prospects, along with numerous other arguments and injuries, propelled Genoa and Venice into major naval battles. The outcomes of these engagements were bloody and savage: prisoners were taken, sometimes killed, and ships were burned and buildings destroyed on both sides. By 1296, just as Marco was beginning to establish himself in the merchant business, war was declared between the rival city-states, and all trade ceased while Venice and Genoa fought to determine who would have supremacy in trading ventures and on the seas.

Though the old family emporiums at Constantinople and Soldaia had been liquidated during the Polos' long absence, Marco began working in the merchant

Marco Polo's image imprinted on a coin. Marco Polo was a popular figure in Venice. People flocked to his house to hear entertaining travel tales.

trade in Venice with the goods he had brought from Asia. In fact the Polos' stock of transportable items had been so huge that they had enough inventory to trade and sell for years. From a Venetian legal document recording that in 1311 Marco Polo pressed charges on another merchant for money owed as the price of some Tibetan sweet musk, we can see that sixteen years after his return to Venice, Marco was still selling items he had brought from Asia.

The Genoese Imprison Marco Polo

With his years of sailing and navigation experience, Marco Polo decided to join the Venetian navy, and he became gentleman commander to a galley. That is, he offered his services as a consultant to the masters of the ship. War galleys in the Venetian fleet were individually owned and maintained by wealthy merchants to protect their harbors and trading ships. These timber vessels had 100 oars on each side and a crew of around 250 men: 40 or 50 men with crossbows, 2 carpenters, several attendants, a cook, and the captain's staff. The Venetian navy boasted about 60 of these ships in all, which were under the command of a single admiral. The navy also had its own doctors, surgeons, armorers, crossbow makers, fletchers (arrow makers), officers of arms and supplies, council of gentlemen, and even musicians to rouse the spirit of the crew in battle and to keep the rowers synchronized with the beat of kettle drums. The ships carried long, colored streamers that blew in the wind and helped citizens of each city-state to recognize vessels in their own fleets.

Three years after his return to Venice, Marco was involved in a naval engagement believed to have taken place off the Dalmatian island of Curzola, on September 7, 1298. In this battle the Genoese captured most of the Venetian fleet, including the ship Marco had sailed on, and Marco and seven thousand of his fellow Venetians were taken prisoner. The admiral of the Venetian fleet was so humiliated by this defeat that rather than allow himself to be captured, he committed suicide by banging his head against a bench. As was customary, the banners of the captured ships were torn down and allowed to drag in the water as the ships were towed backward to port.

In Marco Polo's day, a Venetian war galley might have looked something like this. With his years of sailing experience, Polo became a gentleman commander to a galley.

Tales of Riches

Though Marco Polo never visited Japan and his descriptions of its riches were based on hearsay, Marco made the country (which he believed to consist of a single island) sound so appealing that Columbus was inspired to undertake the voyage that led him, accidentally, to the New World. From this excerpt from Ronald Latham's translation of Marco's book, it is easy to see why so many explorers were inspired by Marco's tales of riches.

"Japan is an island far out at sea to the eastward, some 1,500 miles from the mainland. It is a very big island. The people are fair-complexioned, good-looking, and well-mannered. They are idolaters, wholly independent and exercising no authority over any nation but themselves. They have gold in great abundance, because it is found there in measureless quantities. And I assure you that no one exports it from the island, because no trader, nor indeed anyone else, goes there from the mainland. That is how they come to possess so much of it—so much indeed that I can report to you in sober truth a veritable marvel concerning a certain palace of the ruler of the island. You may take it for a fact that he has a very large palace entirely roofed with fine gold. Just as we roof our houses or churches with lead, so this palace is roofed with fine gold. And the value of it is almost beyond computation. Moreover all the chambers, of which there are many, are likewise paved with fine gold to a depth of more than two fingers' breadth. And the halls and the windows and every other part of the palace are likewise adorned with gold. All in all I can tell you that the palace is of such incalculable richness that any attempt to estimate its value would pass the bounds of the marvellous.

They have pearls in abundance, red in color, very beautiful, large and round. They are worth as much as the white ones, and indeed more. In this island the dead are sometimes buried, sometimes cremated, but everyone who is buried has one of these pearls put in his mouth. Such is the custom that prevails among them. They also have many other precious stones in abundance. It is a very rich island, so that no one could count its riches."

Along with other men of similar rank and social position, Marco was imprisoned in an underground room of the Palazzo di San Giorgio in Genoa, which housed a great many Pisan and Venetian prisoners. Some of the other wealthy prisoners were released in exchange for ransom money, but although Niccolo and Maffeo Polo tried several times to ransom Marco, they were unsuccessful in obtaining his release.

Instead, Marco lived at the prison for more than a year, where he quickly became popular among the other prisoners and among the guards because of his bottomless supply of entertaining stories. The long, boring days in prison were shortened whenever Marco started talking of his adventures in the East. All the men liked to sit near him and listen to descriptions of life at the khan's court and tales of the khan's wives and concubines. Marco became well known in Genoa while imprisoned there, and many of the citizens came to the jail to visit him. Before long his fame entitled him to privileges not normally extended to prisoners. Giambattista Ramusio, who wrote a biography of Marco Polo around 1557, tells of Marco's popularity:

> Because, as may be understood, of his rare qualities and the marvellous voyage which he had made, the whole City [of Genoa] gathered to see him and to talk to him, not treating him as a prisoner, but as a very dear friend and a greatly honored gentleman, and showed him so much honor and affection that there was never an hour of the day that he was not visited by the most noble gentlemen of that city, and presented with everything necessary for his daily life.[54]

Dictating Travel Tales

Marco's stories inspired his cell mate, a Pisan named Rustichello, who had been imprisoned at the Palazzo di San Giorgio since Genoa defeated Pisa at the Battle of Meloria in 1284. A writer of prose narratives featuring the legendary King Arthur, Rustichello wanted Marco to dictate his travel tales so that he could make a book from them. Marco decided that writing a book was an excellent idea, and he asked permission to send to Venice for the notebooks he had filled during his travels. Because of Marco's good relations with the prison guards and his popularity, he was granted this request. When he received the notebooks, he began to dictate from them to Rustichello, who recorded the material on parchment, creating the book Marco called *A Description of the World*.

Rustichello wrote the book primarily in the third person, and in French, which was the diplomatic language of the day and the one spoken at the courts of European royalty. That Rustichello intended the book to be read by royalty is evident in the manuscript's opening line: "Emperors and kings, dukes and marquises, counts, knights, and townsfolk, and all people who wish to know the various races of men and the peculiarities of the various regions of the world, take this book and have it read to you."[55] In the prologue to *A Description of the World*, Rustichello plugs Marco's narrative by adding, in his typically flowery style:

> From the time when our Lord God formed Adam, our first parent, with his hands down to this day there has been no man, Christian or Pagan, Tartar or

Indian, or of any race whatsoever, who has known or explored so many of the various parts of the world and of its great wonders as this same Messer Marco Polo. For this reason he made up his mind that it would be a great pity if he did not have a written record made of all the things he had seen and had heard by true report, so that others who have not seen and do not know them may learn them from this book.[56]

By the time truces were signed between Genoa and Venice and Genoa and Pisa in 1299, freeing Marco and Rustichello, the book had been completed.

A Description of the World

The publication of his book in 1298 gradually brought Marco attention from beyond the city of Venice, where he was already commonly known as "Marco of the millions" because of his excessive use of the word "million" when describing the riches of Kublai Khan. Marco's manuscript was copied numerous times and by the sixteenth century had been translated into many languages, including Latin, German, Spanish, Portuguese, Italian dialects, English, and Gaelic, to satisfy the literate public's desire for knowledge of Eastern customs and culture. During Marco's lifetime the manuscript was translated into Latin and the Italian dialect called Tuscan. In fact, Marco's manuscript became one of the first books printed in Europe, after the invention of the printing press in 1455. *A Description of the World* was a part of the library of every nobleman or scholar.

In the early 1300s Marco was visited by Pietro d'Abano, a well-known professor of medicine at the University of Padua. Pietro had read Marco's book and wanted to ask him questions about the Asian climate and the stars visible in the East. After conversing with Marco, the professor wrote a treatise discussing the existence of a large star visible only from the East and speculating about whether it was possible to live south of the equator, citing Marco as his source. The following excerpt from Professor d'Abano's treatise reflects some early four-

The frontispiece of the first printed edition of Marco Polo's book A Description of the World. *Polo's book was one of the first books printed in Europe after the invention of the printing press.*

teenth-century scientific beliefs about the relation of climate to human size.

About this, together with other matters, Marco the Venetian told me [and he is] the man who has encompassed more of the world in his travels than any I have ever known, and a most diligent investigator. He saw this same star under the Antarctic Pole, and it has a great tail, of which he drew the figure, thus [here follows the drawing]. He told me also that he saw the Antarctic Pole [star] at an altitude above the earth apparently equal to the length of a soldier's lance, and the Arctic Pole

Toscanelli's Map

Marco's mistake in locating Japan 1,500 miles to the east of China was largely responsible for the landing in the New World of Columbus in 1492. A paper published in the Journal of the American Geographical Society *in 1879 explains how this happened.*

"The first step in the direction of rearranging the map of the world was made by Toscanelli, a learned cosmographer of Florence. He constructed a map, now lost, the object of which appears to have been to represent the eastern portion of Asia, and the islands to the east and south of it (a part of the world unknown to Ptolemy, but with which Toscanelli had become acquainted through the travels of Marco Polo and others), and also to show that Asia could be reached by sailing westward from Portugal, directly across the then unknown Atlantic. In 1474, Toscanelli sent this map, accompanied by a letter, to Columbus, to confirm the great discoverer in the design he then entertained of attempting to sail westward across the Atlantic to the Indies. In this map, Toscanelli divided the space between the western shores of Portugal and the eastern part of Asia into twenty-six divisions or spaces of 250 miles each, and probably laid down the eastern part of Asia with Marco Polo's outlying islands of Japan, Java, etc., as they are found on the globe of Martin Behaim, supposed to have been constructed in the year that Columbus discovered America and which geographical information, it has been inferred, Behaim acquired from the map of Toscanelli. . . . This map is supposed to have been projected after the manner of Ptolemy, incorporating the information obtained by Marco Polo."

[star] was hidden. . . . He informs me that the heat there is intense, and the habitations few in number. These things indeed he saw on a certain island at which he arrived by sea. He says, moreover, that the men there are very large . . . and he had found this because in such places one does not meet with the cold of the body which is exhausting and consequently tends to make one smaller.[57]

That a Paduan scholar consulted Marco Polo on scientific matters shows that Marco's knowledge of Eastern geography was recognized and appreciated during his lifetime. Some historians believe the star with "a great tail" that Marco observed was actually the Southern Cross, a constellation visible only from the southern hemisphere. Marco may have been the first European to have recorded observations of these stars. Evidence supporting this claim comes from the work of one of Marco's contemporaries, the Florentine Dante Alighieri. Dante is believed to have referred to the Southern Cross in his *Divine Comedy* ("to the right hand I turn'd, and fix'd my mind/ On the other pole attentive, where I saw/ Four stars ne'er seen before"), which suggests that the poet knew about the stars.[58] When Dante began the *Divine Comedy* in 1308, he could have learned about the existence of such a constellation only from Marco Polo or Professor d'Abano.

In 1307 Charles de Valois, brother of the French king Philip IV, asked Marco for a copy of his manuscript, and Marco sent him one because, in the self-congratulatory words of the note he enclosed with the book, "I am a very honorable person of high character and respect in many countries because of my desire that what I have

witnessed be known throughout the world." Marco's manuscript was in demand during his lifetime, as shown by the Dominican chronicler Francesco Pipino of Bologna, who translated *A Description of the World* into Latin in 1320 "at the urgent request of many Brothers, Fathers, and Masters."[59] Pipino hailed Marco as a champion of the Catholic faith, saying that Marco's book taught readers to admire the "variety, beauty, and immensity of [God's] Creation."

Fame and Notoriety

So Marco's life upon his return to Venice was a mixture of fame and notoriety; while he received recognition and appreciation from scholars, he also met much skepticism and disbelief from his fellow Venetians, whose knowledge of the world was too limited to incorporate Marco's experiences. According to legend, children used to run after Marco calling "Marco, tell us another lie." Marco's tales were too far-fetched for the average person to accept without proof. The citizens of medieval Venice could not know what coal was, and so a report of "stones that burn like logs" was hard to believe. "Marco of the millions" was a nickname that stuck; to this day Marco Polo's old house is known as "Millions Court," and his book is called *Il Milione* in Italy. According to tradition, after Marco's death, clowns at Venetian carnivals dressed up like the merchant-explorer, called themselves Marco Polo, and walked around telling outrageous stories as if they were true.

Few details are known of Marco's life after his release from prison. While he was in his forties, however, he married a

Venetian noblewoman named Donata, who bore him three daughters, Fantina, Bellela, and Moreta. By 1300 Niccolo Polo had died, and sometime after 1310 Marco's uncle Maffeo also died. Marco continued to work at the merchant trade, selling local products like Venetian glass, metal, jewels, and silks, and importing cloth, dyes, medicines, or whatever the market demanded. Although much of his business was conducted with foreigners, Venetian law now forbade direct contact between merchants and exporters, so Marco had to use a middleman, or broker. In addition, trade with foreigners was on a barter basis only; no cash sales were permitted. Thus foreigners had to accept Venetian goods

In Venice, Marco Polo became famous for his extensive knowledge of the world. While most people enjoyed Polo's colorful tales, some thought the stories were too outrageous to be true.

MARCVS POLVS

in payment for their wares. Cash sales were allowed only between Venetian merchants, a practice rigged to their advantage because it helped keep hard currency within the city. Though Marco worked as a merchant for the rest of his life, his later years appear to have been increasingly devoted to the distribution of his book, which he had transcribed numerous times so that he could have a copy ready in case a buyer requested it.

"I Do Not Believe It"

A note attached to a Florentine manuscript of *A Description of the World* by a man who hand copied the work in 1392 reveals the skepticism of the average person toward the book:

> Here ends the book of Messer Marco Polo of Venice, which I, Amelio Bonaguisi wrote with my own hand while Podesta [chief magistrate] of Cierreto Guidi to pass the time and [drive away] melancholy. The contents appear to me to be incredible things and his statements appear to me not lies but more likely miracles. And it may well be true that about which he tells; but I do not believe it, though none the less there are found throughout the world many different things in one country and another. But this [book] seems to me, as I copied it for my pleasure, to be [composed of] matters not to be believed or credited. At least, so I aver for myself. And I finished copying it in the aforementioned Cierreto Guidi on the 12th day of November in the year of the Lord 1392.

And, the book being finished, we give thanks to Christ our Lord, Amen.[60]

Though Marco's book confirmed the travelogues of Giovanni di Plano Carpini and William of Rubrick—Christian missionaries who traveled across Asia to Mongolia in the mid-1200s—one reason *A Description of the World* was not accepted as more than fiction may have been the virtual absence of opportunity to confirm Marco's reports. Shortly after *A Description of the World* was written, the rise of the Ming dynasty in China and the ascendancy of the Turks in the Middle East helped to make travel across Asia difficult, and the Far East once again became inaccessible to Western travelers.

Shortly after A Description of the World *was written, Pope Clement V forbade all trading with Muslims. This, along with other events, discouraged travel in the Middle East.*

In 1307 Pope Clement V forbade all trading with the Muslims, who were considered the enemies of the church. Contracts between Muslims and Venetian and other European traders had traditionally contained the phrase "in the name of the Lord and Muhammed," and the church did not want Christians signing such documents. The pope's decree was largely ineffective, though, because a way to circumvent it was found: many merchants continued to trade with the Muslims, but recanted this sin on their deathbeds and received absolution—in exchange for leaving to the church the wealth they had accumulated. But other events, especially the collapse of the Mongol Empire, helped to discourage travel in the Middle East and to make contact with China impossible.

A Troubled Empire

After his death in 1294, Kublai Khan was succeeded by his son Timur, and then by a number of degenerate descendants. By 1328 civil war had convulsed the Mongolian royal family, and rivalry and internal conflict had weakened the Yuan dynasty of Mongols. Adding to these problems were the continued flooding of the Yellow River and the outbreak of famines in northern China, which caused the peasant population to lose their crops and to rebel against taxation. Meanwhile, peasants in the south of China, whose crops were unaffected by these disasters, were taxed heavily to help compensate for the loss of revenues from the north, and they rebelled as well.

The Chinese had always hated being controlled by the Mongols, and some rebellious Chinese had formed secret societies during the Mongol occupation in the hope of inciting a revolution. In 1368 Chu Yuan-chang, a Buddhist monk, harnessed this Chinese resentment and raised a rebel army that seized Khan-balik and ousted the Mongols from the city. The Chinese announced a return to Chinese rule and an era of isolationism, called the Ming (meaning "brilliant") dynasty. Vehemently antiforeign, the Ming dynasty discouraged trade and cultural contacts with outsiders. By 1382, the last Mongols had been driven from China and forced to retreat to the Mongolian steppes or to other parts of their old empire.

By the mid-1300s the trade routes and silk roads were no longer as safe to travel as they had been when the Mongols patrolled the thoroughfares. With the collapse of the Mongol Empire, the Muslims regained autonomy over the Middle East, and Turkish advances into western Asia in the early 1300s also helped block the overland routes from Europe to the eastern regions of Asia. The Turks adopted Islam and established supremacy in Asia Minor and northern Syria, and within a few years of Marco's return to Venice the Central Asian land routes to the Far East were nearly impassable. Venetian merchants, therefore, could not profit from Marco's journey directly. Nor could adventuresome travelers verify Marco's stories about Asia. The next formal European contact with the Far East would not occur for nearly two-hundred years, when Portuguese explorer Vasco da Gama, inspired by Marco's book, visited India in 1497.

The Death of Marco Polo

When seventy-year-old Marco became ill and was forced to take to his bed, he called for a legal notary, so that he could arrange for the disposal of his property, and for a priest. He dictated his will to the notary, providing that his wife be given enough money to cover all her expenses, as well as all the linens and household furnishings. He also announced that his personal slave, Peter, whom he had brought with him from Asia, should be freed from all conditions of servitude, adding that "I likewise remit to him all that he may have earned by his labors in his own house, and over and above this I bequeath him one hundred lire of Venetian denari."[61] Marco divided the rest of his property equally among his three daughters.

When accused of embellishing his travel tales, Marco Polo replied, "I have not told half of what I saw."

An inventory of Marco's possessions taken at the time of his death shows that Fantina, Bellela, and Moreta inherited a number of exotic items, including a great quantity of expensive cloth in the form of gold and silk brocade coverings and hangings, the golden passport tablet Kublai Khan had given Marco for safe travel in his dominions, and a traditional Mongolian silver belt. There was also a bochta, the ceremonial headdress of Mongol women, which was most likely a gift to Marco upon his departure from Persia from the princess Kokachin. (It was customary to offer a royal garment as a parting gift and as a sign of esteem.) After Marco had bequeathed all his worldly goods, the notary left and the priest performed the last rites of the church.

Some close friends visited Marco on his deathbed and begged him to recant some of his incredible stories so that when he died, his soul could find peace. But Marco's only reply was the resolute response, "I have not told half of what I saw." Sometime after sunset on January 8, 1324, Marco Polo died in bed at his home. He was buried next to his father at the church of San Lorenzo in Venice.

Marco's Legacy

The book *A Description of the World* preserved for future generations a wealth of information about Asian civilization—embracing history, religion, politics, economics, cultural anthropology, zoology, botany, and geography. In the prologue, Rustichello wrote:

> [Marco] made up his mind that it would be a great pity if he did not have a written record made of all the things he had seen and had heard by true report, so that others who have not seen them and do not know them may learn them from this book.[62]

Most historians agree that while the Polos' travels were remarkable, they had very little impact on thirteenth-century Venice or on Marco's other European contemporaries. The real legacy of those travels resides in the historical significance of *A Description of the World*, which eventually helped revise European geography, making the farthest reaches of Asia accessible to Western readers and leading directly to European interest in exploring foreign lands. At a time when Europe had feared foreigners and was suspicious of other races and cultures, Marco's book showed Asians as basically friendly and interested in the West.

A Description of the World became a very popular book over the next couple of cen-

turies, and it interested many readers from all over Europe. The manuscript was hand copied numerous times: approximately 119 manuscript versions have been found in languages ranging from Spanish to Gaelic. *A Description of the World* was one of the first books printed on the movable-

Marco Polo's reports helped revise geographical data and arouse the interest of European explorers.

type press invented by Johannes Gutenberg in 1455, and the first printed copy of Marco's book was a German translation made at Nuremberg in 1477.

Geographical Descriptions

Marco's book provided a rich resource for geographers, who used its descriptions of Asia in two important sets of maps, completed shortly after Marco's death, that revised the medieval conception of the East. Both the Laurentian Atlas (named after Lorenzo de'Medici), completed in 1351, and the Catalan Atlas, completed in 1375, depict Central Asia, East Asia, and parts of India as described by Marco Polo. Both maps attempt to create accurate physical geography based on eyewitness account, rather than folklore or biblical legend. Marco Polo's geographical descriptions became Europe's primary source of information about Asia during the late Middle Ages. Modern travelers who have followed the route of Marco Polo across Asia say that Marco's use of the term "a day's journey" to denote units of distance continues to provide an accurate measurement between cities on the old caravan routes. Even sixteenth-century maps reflect the influence of *A Description of the World*. An early history of cartography mentions that the Roman map of Johann Ruysch, dated 1508, which delineated the internal regions of eastern Asia, was "no longer based on Marinus of Tyre and Ptolemy, . . . but on more modern reports, especially those of Marco Polo."[63]

Perhaps the most significant impact of Marco's book on Europe was its influence on the Italian explorer Christopher

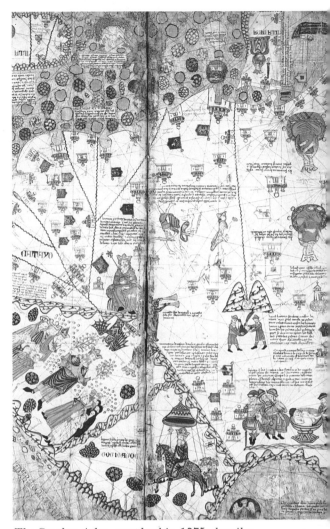

The Catalan Atlas, completed in 1375, describes parts of Asia based on Polo's travels.

Columbus. In *A Description of the World*, Marco reports on Japan as an island overflowing with gold and other sought-after goods, and he also estimates that Japan is 1,500 miles off the eastern coast of China. Marco's generous estimate of the distance of Japan from China, which far exceeded the estimates of earlier geographers, along with his descriptions of the riches to be found in Japan, were crucial in convincing

Christopher Columbus that he could reach the East by sailing west across the Atlantic Ocean. We deduce that Columbus had intended to visit Japan and China because when he set sail for the East via the Atlantic Ocean, he carried a well-marked copy of *A Description of the World*, along with letters from Ferdinand and Isabella of Spain addressed to "the Great Khan of Cathay." Thus Marco Polo's book was instrumental in the European discovery of the New World, for when Columbus set sail for Asia he encountered the western hemisphere, instead.

Columbus was not the only traveler inspired by Marco's descriptions of countries rich in natural resources and such exportable commodities as gold, gems, wood, and spices. A copy of Marco's book was given to the Portuguese royal family in 1428, along with a map copied from one Marco had drawn of his travels in the East. The Portuguese explorer Vasco da Gama, who sailed to India in 1497, was prompted in part by Marco's descriptions of India, and da Gama's successful journey brought renewed attention to Marco's book and faith in its accuracy. Marco's descriptions

Based on A Description of the World, *Christopher Columbus was convinced that he could reach the Orient by sailing west. Instead, he discovered the New World.*

A Description of the World *prompted Portuguese explorer Vasco da Gama to sail to India in 1497. Da Gama's trip verified the accuracy of information in the book.*

of the wealth of China, Japan, Sumatra, and India provided an incentive for numerous explorers, including the Spanish conquistadors, and England's Sir Francis Drake and Sir Walter Raleigh.

A Description of the World helped dissolve the medieval "ne plus ultra" (go no further) mindset typified in Dante's *Divine Comedy,* in which the explorer Ulysses resides in Hell, punished by God for having attempted to sail past the Strait of Gibraltar (thereafter known as the Pillars of Hercules) into the Atlantic Ocean and parts unknown. With the help of books like *A Description of the World,* Europe shifted from the medieval attitude that man should not exceed certain limits to the Renaissance notion of human skill and brawn. This shift is perhaps best exemplified by Charles V, a ruler of the Holy Roman Empire, who in 1519 minted coins of gold taken from Peru that featured the Pillars of Hercules, with the motto "plus," meaning "more," stamped below.

Marco's geographical descriptions of the world were crucial in pushing Europe into an age of exploration, inspired by the belief that man has the power to explore his environment, a belief that ultimately led to an era of colonialism, during which Europe attempted to spread its control and influence to other parts of the world.

Notes

Introduction: Forerunner of an International Age

1. Cottie A. Burland, *The Travels of Marco Polo*. New York: McGraw-Hill, 1970.

Chapter 1: A World in Transition

2. Richard Humble, *Marco Polo*. London: Weidenfeld and Nicolson, 1975.
3. Quoted in Rebecca Stefoff, *Marco Polo and the Medieval Explorers*. New York: Chelsea House, 1992.
4. Ezekiel 5:5.
5. Stefoff, *Marco Polo and the Medieval Explorers*.
6. Stefoff, *Marco Polo and the Medieval Explorers*.
7. Stefoff, *Marco Polo and the Medieval Explorers*.
8. Quoted in Manuel Komroff, ed., *The Travels of Marco Polo*. New York: Boni and Liverwright, 1926.

Chapter 2: The First Journey of the Polos

9. Henry H. Hart, *Marco Polo: Venetian Adventurer*. Stanford, CA: Stanford University Press, 1942.
10. Quoted in Hart, *Venetian Adventurer*.
11. Quoted in Hart, *Venetian Adventurer*.
12. Quoted in Ronald Latham, transl. and ed., *The Travels of Marco Polo*. London: Penguin Books, 1958.
13. Leonardo Olschki, *Marco Polo's Asia* (transl. John L. Scott). Berkeley: University of California Press, 1960.

Chapter 3: The Second Journey of the Polos

14. Quoted in Hart, *Venetian Adventurer*.
15. Quoted in Maria Bellonci, transl., and Teresa Waugh, ed., *The Travels of Marco Polo*. New York: Facts on File, 1984.
16. Latham, *The Travels*.
17. Quoted in Robert Silverburg, *The Realm of Prester John*. Garden City, NY: Doubleday, 1972.
18. Latham, *The Travels*.
19. Hart, *Venetian Adventurer*.
20. Quoted in Latham, *The Travels*.
21. Dante, quoted in Olschki, *Marco Polo's Asia*.
22. Quoted in Hart, *Venetian Adventurer*.
23. Quoted in Hart, *Venetian Adventurer*.
24. Latham, *The Travels*.
25. Quoted in Hart, *Venetian Adventurer*.
26. Latham, *The Travels*.
27. Quoted in Hart, *Venetian Adventurer*.

Chapter 4: Khan-Balik: At the Court of the Great Khan

28. Sir Percy Sykes, *The Quest for Cathay*. London: A. & C. Black, 1936.
29. Quoted in Hart, *Venetian Adventurer*.
30. Latham, *The Travels*.
31. Latham, *The Travels*.
32. Latham, *The Travels*.
33. Quoted in Komroff, *The Travels*.
34. Quoted in Hart, *Venetian Adventurer*.
35. Latham, *The Travels*.
36. Latham, *The Travels*.
37. Latham, *The Travels*.
38. Olschki, *Marco Polo's Asia*.

Chapter 5: Escape from Khan-Balik

39. Quoted in Henry H. Hart, *A Garden of Peonies*. Stanford, CA: Stanford University Press, 1938.
40. Quoted in Hart, *Venetian Adventurer*.
41. Latham, *The Travels*.
42. Hart, *Venetian Adventurer*.
43. Latham, *The Travels*.
44. Latham, *The Travels*.
45. Latham, *The Travels*.
46. Latham, *The Travels*.
47. Latham, *The Travels*.
48. Latham, *The Travels*.
49. Latham, *The Travels*.
50. Latham, *The Travels*.
51. Quoted in Burland, *The Travels*.

Chapter 6: Back in Venice

52. Quoted in Hart, *Venetian Adventurer*.
53. Quoted in Hart, *Venetian Adventurer*.
54. Quoted in Hart, *Venetian Adventurer*.
55. Latham, *The Travels*.
56. Latham, *The Travels*.
57. Quoted in Hart, *Venetian Adventurer*.
58. Dante, *The Divine Comedy*, quoted in Antionio Giordano, *Marco Polo and After*. New York: Adelaide Press, 1974.
59. Quoted in Hart, *Venetian Adventurer*.
60. Quoted in Hart, *Venetian Adventurer*.
61. Quoted in Hart, *Venetian Adventurer*.

Epilogue: Marco's Legacy

62. Quoted in Latham, *The Travels*.
63. Hart, *Venetian Adventurer*.

For Further Reading

Cottie A. Burland, *The Travels of Marco Polo*. New York: McGraw-Hill, 1970. The narrative format of this book makes it interesting to read, and the reader also learns what was happening in Europe at the time of the Polos' travels.

Henry H. Hart, *Marco Polo: Venetian Adventurer*. Stanford, CA: Stanford University Press, 1942. This biography of Marco Polo records many details of his life as well as information on Venetian history during Polo's lifetime and the impact of *A Description of the World* on subsequent generations in Europe.

R.I. Moore, general editor, *Rand McNally Atlas of World History*. New York: Rand McNally, 1983. Maps of the ancient and modern worlds, with accounts of what was going on at the same time in different regions. This atlas is helpful for understanding the balance of power among Muslims, Christians, and Mongols in the Middle East. Also an indispensable resource for those interested in world history.

Michael Prawdin, *The Mongol Empire*. New York: Macmillan, 1940. An extensive history of the Mongols, beginning with the rise of Genghis Khan and concluding with the legacy of the Mongols to Asia. For those who want to know more about the Mongols and their empire, this is an excellent source.

Susan Roth, *Marco Polo's Notebook*. Garden City, NY: Doubleday, 1991. A short, beautifully illustrated book with an emphasis on ancient geography; a record of the journey of the Polos across Asia.

Rebecca Stefoff, *Marco Polo and the Medieval Explorers*. New York: Chelsea House, 1992. A broad overview of Marco Polo's journey and the travels of such other explorers as Ibn Batuta.

Additional Works Consulted

Juliet Bredon, *Peking*. Shanghai: Kelly and Walsh, 1922. Good physical descriptions of ancient Peking, including maps of the city under the Mongol occupation.

Cottie A. Burland, *The Travels of Marco Polo*. New York: McGraw-Hill, 1970. The Polo story in an almost narrative format, set in the historical context of Europe in the late Middle Ages.

Christopher Dawson, *The Mongol Missions*. London: Sheed and Ward, 1955. Excellent source on early papal missions to the Mongol Empire by friars, the precursors of the Polos, especially Giovanni de Plano Carpini and William of Rubrick.

Leonardo Olschki, *Marco Polo's Asia*. Berkeley: University of California Press, 1960. Highly detailed, scholarly work on the cultural aspects of the Polos' journeys to Asia, specifically on what Marco's book has meant for scholars of Asian history, anthropologists, and other specialists.

Robert Silverburg, *The Realm of Prester John*. Garden City, NY: Doubleday, 1972. Fascinating and humorous account of Europe's search through Asia, the Middle East, and Africa for the Christian empire of Prester John.

Sir Percy Sykes, *The Quest for Cathay*. London: A. & C. Black, 1936. Details historic European attempts to penetrate Asia. Also chronicles Asian explorers in the Middle East and the Roman world. A witty book, full of literary and historical insights.

H.G. Wells, *The Outline of History*, Vol. II. New York: Garden City Publishing Company, 1930. Manages to condense thousands of years of history into two volumes, but offers much commentary on the Mongol military.

Editions of *The Travels* consulted:

Maria Bellonci, transl., and Teresa Waugh, ed., *The Travels of Marco Polo*. New York: Facts on Files, 1984.

Richard Humble, *Marco Polo*. London: Weidenfeld and Nicolson, 1975.

Manuel Komroff, ed., *The Travels of Marco Polo*. New York: Boni and Liverwright, 1926. Editor's introduction contains much useful and pertinent historical information, including quotations.

Ronald Latham, transl. and ed., *The Travels of Marco Polo*. London: Penguin Books, 1958. Helpful introduction. Gives the historiography of the editions of the travels and supplies modern place names in addition to ancient place names.

H. Murray, ed., *The Travels of Marco Polo*. New York: Harper Bros., 1845.

Index

Credits

Cover photo by North Wind Picture Archives

Archiv für Kunst und Geschichte, Berlin, 11, 41, 52, 74

Art Resource, 60

The Bettmann Archive, 16, 17, 30, 49, 61, 84

Bibliotheque Nationale, 18(bottom), 32, 63(top), 64(top), 68, 85

Bodleian Library, 58, 64(bottom)

Bridgeman/Art Resource, 47

Culver Pictures, Inc., 56, 70

Giraudon/Art Resource, 27, 69, 80

Library of Congress, 12, 86

North Wind Picture Archives, 15(bottom), 22, 28, 40, 42, 43(bottom), 44

Stock Montage, Inc., 10, 13, 15(top), 23, 24, 29, 35, 38, 39, 43(top), 45, 46, 48, 51, 53, 57, 63(bottom), 66, 73, 77, 81, 82, 87

Grateful acknowledgment is made to the following for permission to quote from copyrighted sources: From *Marco Polo: Venetian Adventurer* by Henry H. Hart. Copyright © 1967 by the University of Oklahoma Press. Reprinted with permission. From *The Travels of Marco Polo*, Ronald Latham, trans. London: Penguin, 1958. Copyright © Ronald Latham, 1958. Reproduced by permission of Penguin Books, Ltd.

About the Author

Mary Hull is a student at Brown University, where she is concentrating in American history. In recent years she has received a grant from the National Endowment for the Humanities, and she has written a biography of Rosa Parks.